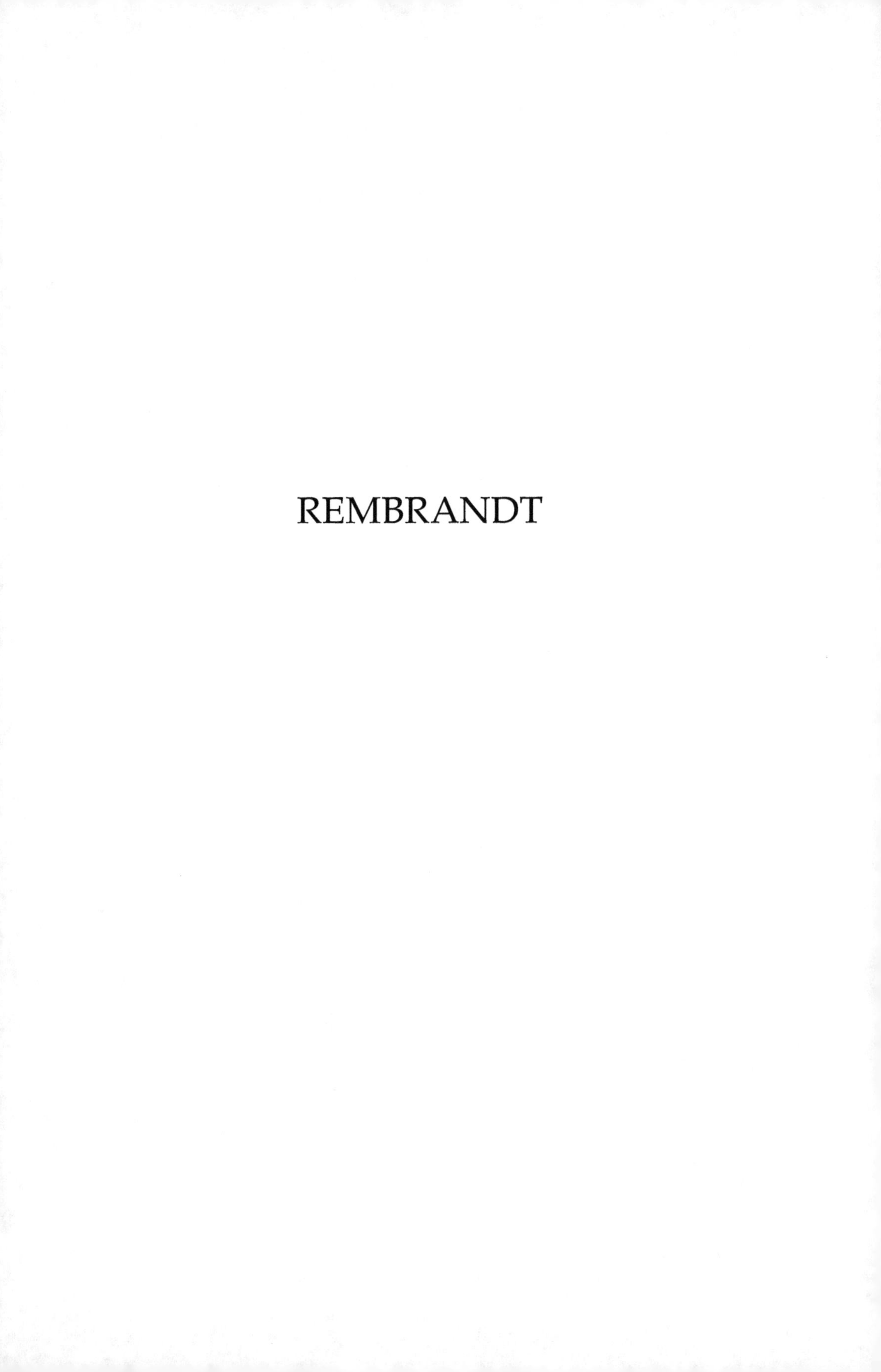

REMBRANDT

REMBRANDT

JOSEF ISRAELS

CRESCENT MOON

First published 1908. This edition © 2018.

Printed and bound in the U.S.A.
Set in Book Antiqua 10 on 14pt.
Designed by Radiance Graphics.

British Library Cataloguing in Publication data

ISBN-13 9781861716347

CRESCENT MOON PUBLISHING
P.O. Box 1312, Maidstone, Kent, ME14 5XU
Great Britain, www.crmoon.com

CONTENTS

NOTE ON THE TEXT

The text is from *Rembrandt* by Josef Israels, published by Frederick A. Stokes, New York City, 1908.

The illustrations in the original text are included in the illustrations section, along with many other works.

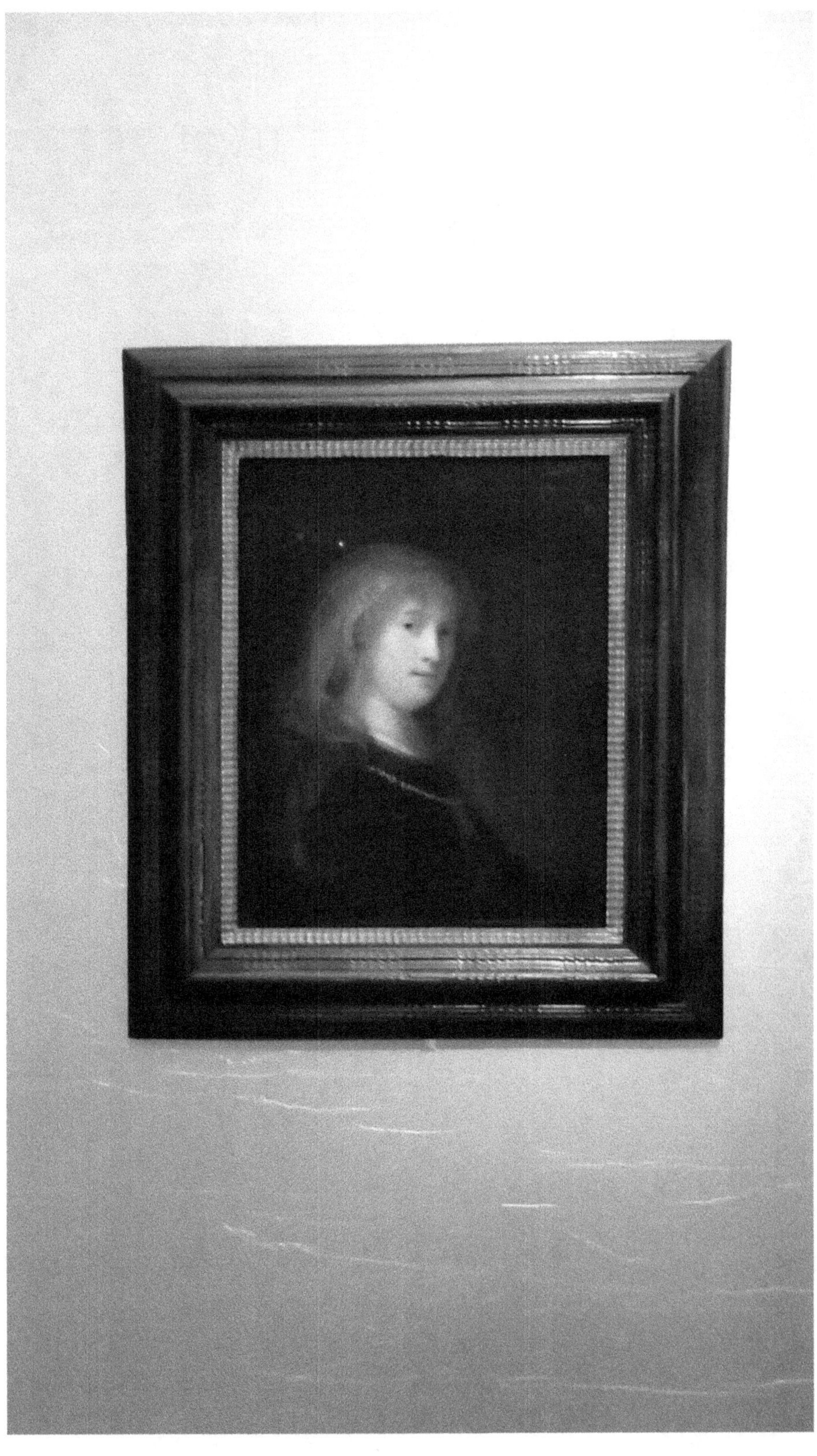

Rembrandt, Self-Portrait, Amsterdam

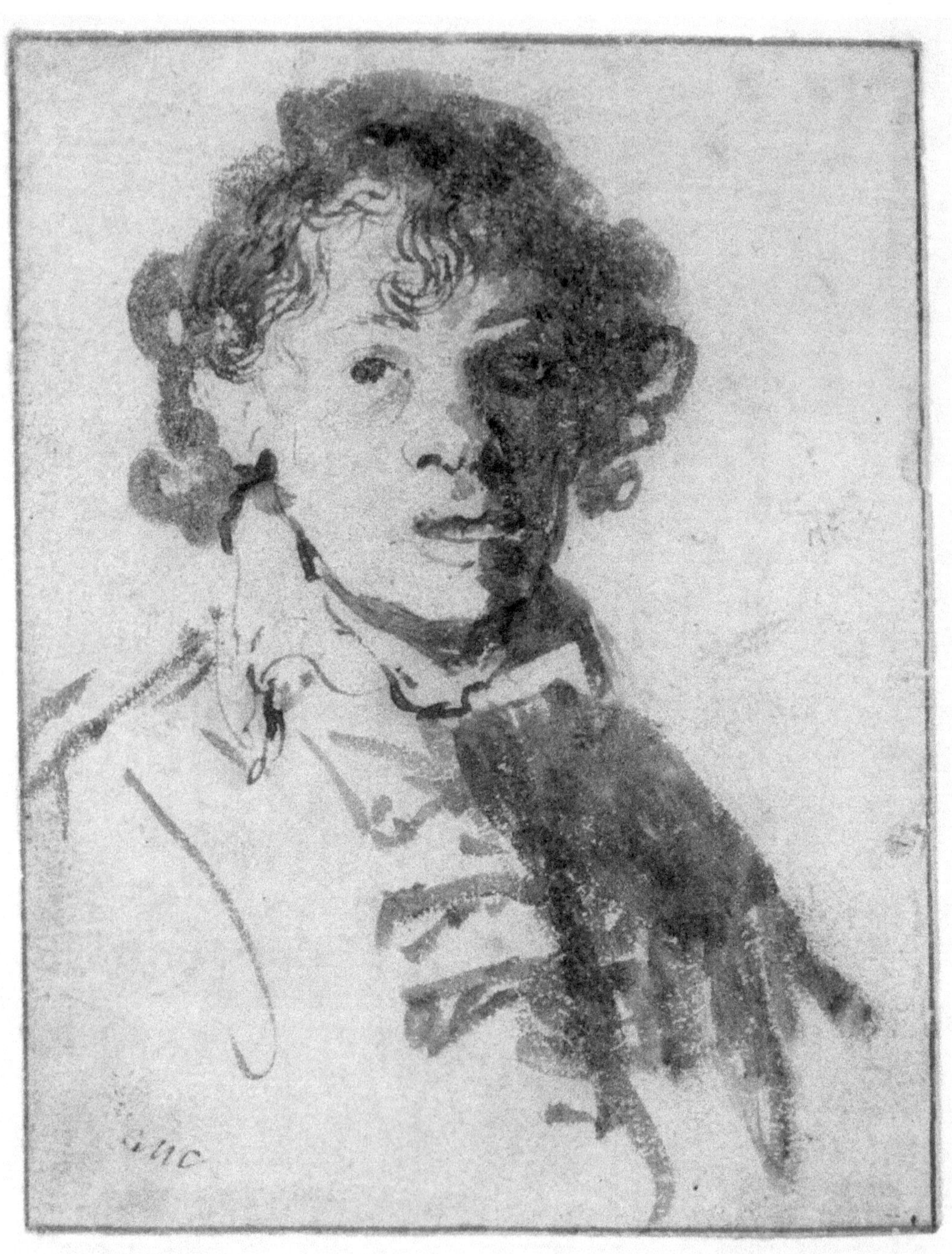

Rembrandt van Rijn, Self-Portrait With Open Mouth, 1629, British Museum

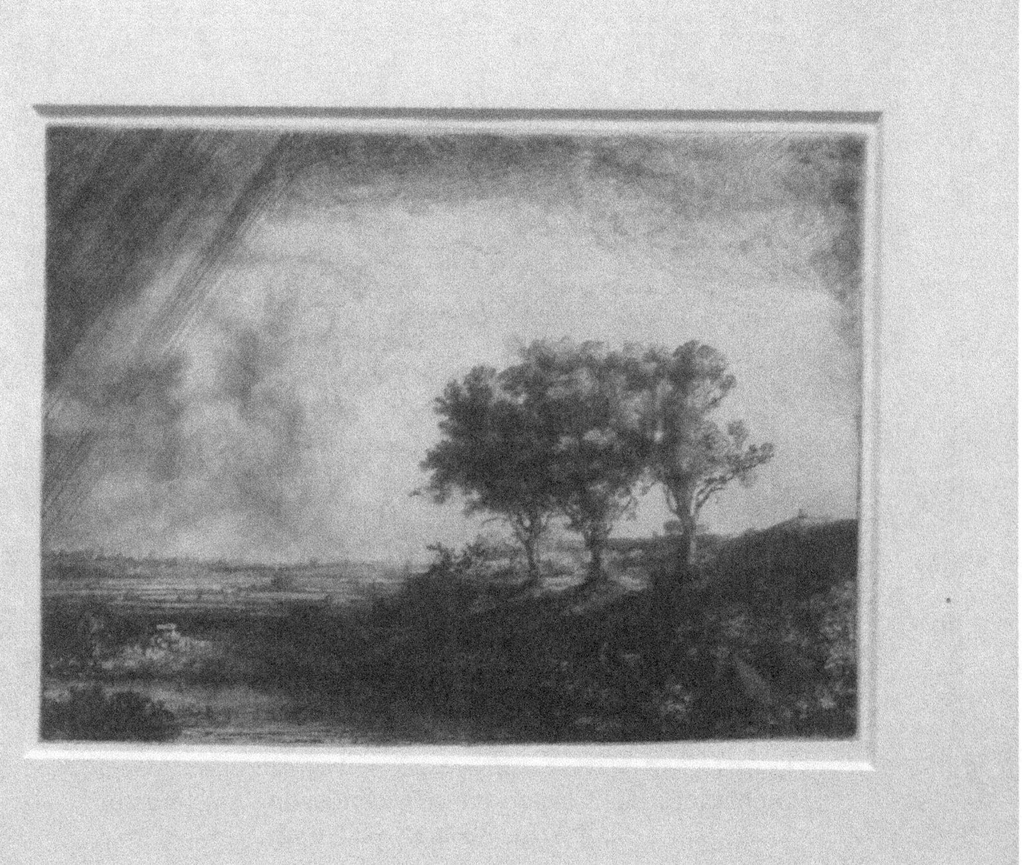

Rembrandt, Three Trees

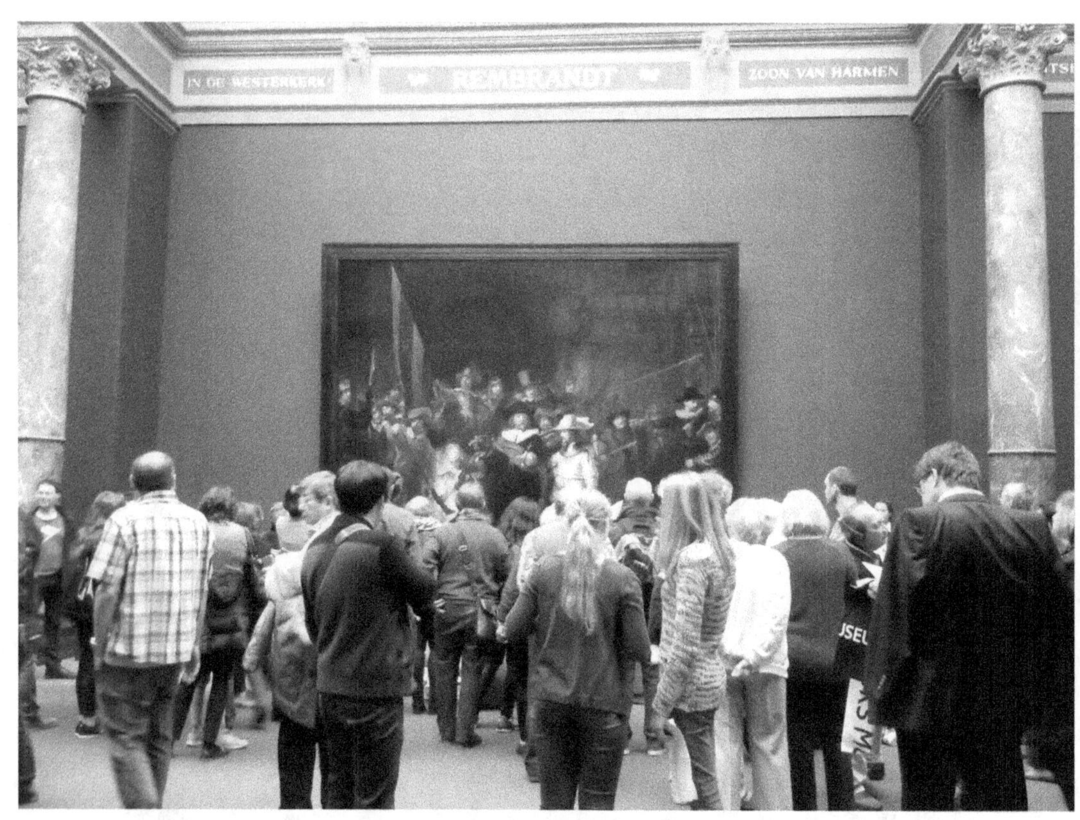

Rembrandt's Night Watch in the Rijksmuseum, Amsterdam
(photo: J. Robinson, 2015)

INTRODUCTION

While the world pays respectful tribute to Rembrandt the artist, it has been compelled to wait until comparatively recent years for some small measure of reliable information concerning Rembrandt the man. The sixteenth and seventeenth centuries seem to have been very little concerned with personalities. A man was judged by his work which appealed, if it were good enough, to an ever-increasing circle. There were no newspapers to record his doings and, if he chanced to be an artist, it was nobody's business to set down the details of his life. Sometimes a diarist chanced to pass by and to jot down a little gossip, quite unconscious of the fact that it would serve to stimulate generations yet unborn, but, for the most part, artists who did great work in a retiring fashion and were not honoured by courts and princes as Rubens was, passed from the scene of their labours with all the details of their sojourn unrecorded.

Rembrandt was fated to suffer more than mere neglect, for he seems to have been a light-hearted, headstrong, extravagant man, with no capacity for business. He had not even the supreme quality, associated in doggerel with Dutchmen, of giving too little and asking too much. Consequently, when he died poor and enfeebled, in years when his collection of works of fine art had been sold at public auction for a fraction of its value, when his pictures had been seized for debt, and wife, mistress, children, and many friends had passed, little was said about him. It was only when the superlative quality of his art was recognised beyond a small circle of admirers that people began to gather up such fragments of biography as they could find.

Shakespeare has put into Mark Antony's mouth the statement that "the evil that men do lives after them," and this was very much the case with Rembrandt van Ryn. His first biographers seem to have no memory save for his undoubted recklessness, his extravagance, and his debts. They remembered that his pictures fetched very good prices, that his studio was besieged for some years by more sitters than it could accommodate, that he was honoured with commissions from the ruling house, and that in short, he had every chance that would have led a good business man to prosperity and an old age removed from stress and strain. These facts seem to have aroused their ire. They have assailed his memory with invective that does not stop short at false statement. They have found in the greatest of all Dutch artists a ne'er-do-well who could not take advantage of his opportunities, who had the extravagance of a company promoter, an explosive temper and all the instincts that make for loose living.

Alas for these poor biographers, who, had they but taken the trouble to trust to the pictures rather than to the lies that were current, would have seen that the artist's life could not have been nearly as bad as they imagined. Happily, to-day, we have more than the testimony of the painted canvas, though that would suffice the most of intelligent men. Further investigation has done a great deal to remove the blemishes from Rembrandt's name; MM. Vosmaer and Michel have restored it as though it were a discoloured picture, and those who hail Rembrandt master may do so without mental reservation. His faults were very human ones and his merits leave them in the shade.

Rembrandt was born in the pleasant city of Leyden, but it is not easy to name the precise year. Somewhere between 1604 and 1607 he started his troubled journey through life, and of his childhood the records are scanty. Doubtless, his youthful imagination was stirred by the sights of the city, the barges moving slowly along the canals, the windmills that were never at rest, the changing chiaroscuro of the flooded, dyke-seamed land. Perhaps he saw these things with the large eye of the artist, for he could not have turned to any point of the compass without finding a picture lying ready for treatment. Even when he was a little boy the fascination of his surroundings may have been responsible in part for the fact that he was not an industrious scholar, that he looked upon reading and writing as rather troublesome accomplishments, worth less than the labour involved in their acquisition. And yet his father was a wealthy man, he would seem to have had no occasion to neglect his studies, and the best one can find to say about these early years is that they may have been directed badly by those in authority. In any case, it is well-nigh impossible to make rules for genius. The boy who sits unmoved at the bottom of his class, the butt of his companions, the horrible example to whom the master turns when he wishes to point a moral, may do work in the world that no one among those who attended the school since its foundation has been able to accomplish and, if Rembrandt did not satisfy his masters, he was at least paving the way for accomplishment that is recognised gratefully to-day wherever art has found a home.

His family soon knew that he had the makings of an artist and, in 1620, when he could hardly have been more than sixteen, and may have been considerably less, he left Leyden University for the studio of a second-rate painter called Jan van Swanenburch. We have no authentic record of his progress in the studio, but it must have been rapid. He must have made friends, painted pictures, and attracted attention. At the end of three years he went to Lastman's studio in Amsterdam, returning thence to Leyden, where he took Gerard Dou as a pupil. A few years later, it is not easy to settle these dates on a satisfactory basis, he went to Amsterdam, and established himself there, because the Dutch capital was very wealthy and held many patrons of the arts, in spite of the seemingly endless war that Holland was waging with

Spain.

The picture of "St. Paul in Prison" would seem to have been produced about 1627, but the painter's appearance before the public of Amsterdam in the guise of an accomplished artist whose work had to be reckoned with, may be said to have dated from the completion of the famous "Anatomy Lesson," in 1631 or 1632. At this time he was living on the Bloemgracht. Rembrandt had painted many portraits when the picture of the medical men and the cadaver created a great sensation and, if we remember that he could not have been more than twenty-seven years old, and may have been no more than twenty-five, it is not difficult to understand that Amsterdam was stirred from its usual reserve, and greeted the rising star with enthusiasm. In a few weeks the entrance to the painter's studio was besieged by people wishing to sit for their portraits, by pupils who brought 100 florins, no small sum in those days for the privilege of working for a year in the master's studio. It may be mentioned here that even in the days when the painter's popularity with the general public of Holland had waned, there was never any lack of enthusiastic students from many countries, all clamouring for admission to the studio.

Many a man can endure adversity with courage; success is a greater trial. Bad times often avail to bring out what is best in creative genius; success tends to destroy it. Rembrandt did not remain unaffected by the quick response that Amsterdam made to his genius. His art remained true and sincere, he declined to make the smallest concession to what silly sitters called their taste, but he did not really know what to do with the money and commissions that flowed in upon him so freely. The best use he made of changing circumstances was to become engaged to Saskia van Uylenborch, the cousin of his great friend Hendrick van Uylenborch, the art dealer of Amsterdam. Saskia, who was destined to live for centuries, through the genius of her husband, seems to have been born in 1612, and to have become engaged to Rembrandt when she was twenty. The engagement followed very closely upon the patronage of Rembrandt by Prince Frederic Henry, the Stadtholder, who instructed the artist to paint three pictures. There seemed no longer any need to hesitate, and only domestic troubles seem to have delayed the marriage until 1634. Saskia is enshrined in many pictures. She is seen first as a young girl, then as a woman. As a bride, in the picture now at Dresden, she sits upon her husband's knee, while he raises a big glass with his outstretched arm. Her expression here is rather shy, as if she deprecated the situation and realised that it might be misconstrued. This picture gave offence to Rembrandt's critics, who declared that it revealed the painter's taste for strong drink and riotous living – they could see nothing more in canvas than a story. Several portraits of Saskia remained to be painted. She would seem to have aged rapidly, for after marriage her days were not long in the land. She was only thirty when she died, and looked considerably older.

In the first years of his married life Rembrandt moved to the Nieuwe Doelstraat. For the time he had more commissions than he knew how to execute, few troubles save those that his fiery temperament provoked, and one great sorrow, arising out of the death of his first-born. There can be no doubt at all that he spent far too much money in these years; he would attend the sales of works of art and pay extravagant sums for any that took his fancy. If he ever paused to question himself, he would be content to explain that he paid big prices in order to show how great was his respect for art and artists. He came to acquire a picture by Rubens, a book of drawings by Lucas van Leyden, and the splendid pearls that may be seen in the later portraits of Saskia. Very soon his rash and reckless methods became known to the dealers, who would push the prices up with the certain knowledge that Rembrandt would rush in where wiser buyers feared to tread. The making of an art collection, the purchase of rich jewels for his wife, together with good and open-handed living, soon began to play havoc with Rembrandt's estate. The artist's temperament offended many of the sober Dutchmen who could not understand it at all, his independence and insistence upon the finality of his own judgment were more offensive still, and after 1636 there were fewer applications for portraits.

In 1638 we find Rembrandt taking an action against one Albert van Loo, who had dared to call Saskia extravagant. It was, of course, still more extravagant of Rembrandt to waste his money on lawyers on account of a case he could not hope to win, but this thought does not seem to have troubled him. He did not reflect that it would set the gossips talking more cruelly than ever. Still full of enthusiasm for life and art, he was equally full of affection for Saskia, whose hope of raising children seemed doomed to disappointment, for in addition to losing the little Rombertus, two daughters, each named Cornelia, had died soon after birth. In 1640 Rembrandt's mother died. Her picture remains on record with that of her husband, painted ten years before, and even the biographers of the artist do not suggest that Rembrandt was anything but a good son. A year later the well-beloved Saskia gave birth to the one child who survived the early years, the boy Titus. Then her health failed, and in 1642 she died, after eight years of married life that would seem to have been happy. In this year Rembrandt painted the famous "Night Watch," a picture representing the company of Francis Banning Cocq, and incidentally a day scene in spite of its popular name. The work succeeded in arousing a storm of indignation, for every sitter wanted to have equal prominence in the canvas. They had subscribed equally to the cost, and Rembrandt had dared to compose the picture!

It may be said that after his wife's death, and the exhibition of this fine work, Rembrandt's pleasant years came to an end. He was then somewhere between thirty-six and thirty-eight years old, he had made his mark, and enjoyed a very large measure of recognition, but henceforward, his career was destined to be a very troubled one, full of disappointment, pain, and care. Perhaps it would have been no bad thing for him if he could have gone with Saskia into the outer darkness. The world would have been poorer, but the man himself would have been spared many years that perhaps even the devoted labours of his studio could not redeem.

Saskia's estate, which seems to have been a considerable one, was left to Rembrandt absolutely, in trust for the sole surviving child Titus, but Rembrandt, after his usual free and easy fashion, did not trouble about the legal side of the question. He did not even make an inventory of the property belonging to his wife, and this carelessness led to endless trouble in future years, and to the distribution of a great part of the property into the hands of gentlemen learned in the law. Perhaps the painter had other matters to think about, he could no longer disguise from himself the fact that public patronage was falling off. It may be that the war with Spain was beginning to make people in comfortable circumstances retrench, but it is more than likely that the artist's name was not known favourably to his fellow-citizens. His passionate temperament and his quick eye for truly artistic effects could not be tolerated by the sober, stodgy men and women who were the rank and file of Amsterdam's comfortable classes. To be sure, the Stadtholder continued his patronage; he ordered the famous "Circumcision" and the "Adoration of the Shepherds." Pupils continued to arrive, too, in large numbers, many of them coming from beyond Holland; but the public stayed away.

Rembrandt was not without friends, who helped him as far as they could, and advised him as much as they dared; but he seems to have been a man who could not be assisted, because in matters of art he allowed no outside interference, and he was naturally impulsive. Money ran through his hands like water through a sieve, though it is only fair to point out that he was very generous, and could not lend a deaf ear to any tale of distress.

Between 1642, when Saskia died, and 1649, it is not easy to follow the progress of his life; we can only state with certainty that his difficulties increased almost as quickly as his work ripened. His connection with Hendrickje Stoffels would seem to have started about 1649, and this woman with whom he lived until her death some thirteen years later, has been abused by many biographers because she was the painter's mistress. Some have endeavoured to prove, without any evidence, that he married her, but this concession to Mrs. Grundy seems a little beside the mark. The relations between the pair were a matter for their own consideration, and it is clear that Hendrickje came to the painter in the time of his greatest trouble, to serve him lovingly and faithfully until she passed away at the comparatively early age of thirty-six.

She bore him two children, who seem to have died young, and, curiously enough, her position in the house was accepted by young Titus Rembrandt, who, when he was nearing man's estate, started, in partnership with her, to deal in pictures and works of art – a not very successful attempt to support the establishment in comfort.

In the year when Hendrickje joined Rembrandt, he could no longer pay instalments on the house he had bought for himself in the Joden Breestraat. About the following year he began to sell property, hoping against hope that he would be able to tide over the bad times. Three years later he started borrowing on a very extensive scale. In 1656 a fresh guardian was appointed for Titus, to whom his father transferred some property, and in that year the painter was adjudged bankrupt. The year 1657 saw much of his private property sold, but his collection of pictures and engravings found comparatively few bidders, and realised no more than 5000 florins. A year later his store of pictures came under the hammer, and in 1660, Hendrickje and Titus started their plucky attempt to establish a little business, in order that they might restore some small part of the family fortune.

For a little time the keen edge of trouble seems to have been turned. One of Rembrandt's friends secured him the commission to paint the "Syndics of the Drapers' Guild," and this is one of the last works of importance in the artist's life, because his sight was beginning to fail. To understand why this fresh trouble fell upon him, it is necessary to turn for a moment to consider the marvellous etchings he produced between 1628 and 1661. The drawings may be disregarded in this connection, though there are about a thousand undisputed ones in existence, but the making of the etchings, of which some two hundred are allowed by all competent observers to be the work of the master, must have inflicted enormous strain upon his sight. When he was passing from middle age, overwhelmed with trouble of every description, it is not surprising that his eyes should have refused to serve him any longer.

One might have thought that the immortals had finished their sport with Rembrandt, but apparently their resources are quite inexhaustible. One year after the state of his eyes had brought etching to an end, the faithful Hendrickje died. A portrait of her, one of the last of the master's works, may be seen in Berlin. The face is a charming and sympathetic one, and moves the observer to a feeling of sympathy that makes the mere question of the Church's participation in her relations with Rembrandt a very small affair indeed.

In the next seven years the old painter passed quietly down towards the great silence. A few ardent admirers among the young men, a few old friends whom no adversity could shake, remained to bring such comfort as they might. With failing sight and health he moved to the Lauriergracht, and the capacity for work came nearly to an end. The lawyers made merry with the various suits. Some had been instituted to recover money that the painter had borrowed, others to settle the vexed question of the creditors' right to Saskia's estate. In 1665 Titus received the balance that was left, when the decision of the courts allowed him to handle what legal ingenuity had not been able to impound.

In the summer of 1668, when he was about twenty-seven years old, Titus married his cousin Magdellena, and this little celebration may be supposed to have cheered the elder Rembrandt a little, but his pleasure was brief, for the young bridegroom died in September of the same year, and in the following year a posthumous daughter was born.

By this time the immortals had completed their task, there was nothing left for them to do; they had broken the old painter's health and his heart, they had reduced him to poverty. So they gave him half a year to digest their gifts, and then some word of pity seems to have entered into their councils, and one of the greatest painters the world has seen was set free from the intolerable burden of life. From certain documents still extant we learn that he was buried at the expense of thirteen florins. He has left to the world some five or six hundred pictures that are admitted to be genuine, together with the etchings and drawings to which reference has been made. He is to be seen in many galleries in the Old World and the New, for he painted his own portrait more than a score of times. Saskia, too, may be seen in several galleries and Hendrickje has not been forgotten.

There is no doubt that many of Rembrandt's troubles were self-inflicted; but his punishment was largely in excess of his sins. His pictures may be admired in nearly all great public collections; they are distributed, too, among private galleries. Rembrandt's art has found a welcome in all countries. We know now that part of his temporary unpopularity in Holland was due to the fact that he was far in advance of his own time, that the conventions of lesser men repelled him, and he was perhaps a little too vigorous in the expression of his opinions. Now, in the years when the voice of fame cannot reach him and his worst detractors are silent, he is set on a pedestal by the side of Velazquez and Titian.

REMBRANDT

AN APPRECIATION OF THE PICTURES IN AMSTERDAM

Will the reader turn away with a shrug of the shoulder, when he sees, heading this essay, the famous name that we hear so often?

I feel like one sitting among friends at a banquet, and though many of the guests have expressed and analysed the same feelings in different toasts, I will not be restrained from expressing, in my turn, my delight in the festive gathering. I touch my glass to ensure a hearing, and I speak as my heart prompts me. It is not very important or interesting, but I am speaking in praise of him in whose honour the feast is given.

In this frame of mind I am contributing my little share to the pile of written matter, which has been produced from all quarters, in honour of the great painter.

I

Many years ago I went to Amsterdam as an art student, to be trained under the auspices of the then famous portrait painter Kruseman. Very soon I was admitted to the master's studio, and beheld with admiration the portraits of the distinguished personages he was painting at the time.

The pink flesh-tints of the faces, the delicate treatment of the draperies and dresses, more often than not standing out against a background of dark red velvet, attracted me immensely.

When, however, I expressed a desire to be allowed to copy some of these portraits, the master refused my request. "No," he said; "if you want to copy, go to the museum in the 'Trippenhuis.'"[1]

I dared not show the bitter disappointment this refusal caused me. Having come fresh from the country, the old masters were a sealed book to me. I failed to discover any beauty in the homely, old-fashioned scenes of dark landscapes over which people went into ecstasies. To my untrained eyes the exhibition in "Arti"[2]

---

1 The "Trippenhuis" was used as a picture gallery before the Ryksmuseum was built. It was an old patrician family mansion belonging to the Trip family. Several members of this family filled important posts in the government of the old Republic of the United Provinces, and some were burgomasters of Amsterdam.

2 "Arti et Amicitiæ" is a society of modern Dutch painters. Occasionally the members organise exhibitions of the work of contemporary countrymen or of foreign artists, and every year there is an exhibition of their own works. These shows are held in the society's own building in Amsterdam at the corner of the "Rokin" and "Spui."

seemed infinitely more beautiful; and Pieneman, Gallait, Calame, and Koekoek especially excited my admiration.

I was not really lacking in artistic instinct any more than my fellow-students, but I had not yet gained the experience and practice, which are indispensable to the true understanding of the quaint but highly artistic qualities of the old Dutch masters. I maintain that however intelligent a man may be, it is impossible to appreciate old Dutch art to the full, or even to enjoy it, unless one has become thoroughly familiar with it, and has tried to identify oneself with it. In order to be able to sound the real character and depth of manifestations of art, the artistic sensibility has to be trained and developed.

It was long before I could summon up sufficient courage to enter this Holy of Holies armed with my colours and brushes. Indeed I only started on this venture after a long spell of hard work, out-of-doors as well as in the studio, and after having made many studies from the nude, and many more still-life studies; then a light broke in upon my darkness.

I began to understand at last that the true aim of art does not consist in the smooth and delicate plastering of the colours. I realised that my chief study was to be the exact value of light and shade, the relief of the objects, and the attitude, movements, and gestures of the figures.

Having learned to look upon art from this point of view, I entered the old "Trippenhuis" with pleasure. Little by little the beauty and truth of these admirable old masters dawned upon me. I perceived that their simple subjects grew rich and full of meaning through the manner in which they were treated. The artists were geniuses, and the world around them either ignored the fact, or did not see it until too late.

Knowing little of art, I chose for my first copy a small canvas, a "Hermit" by Gerard Dou, not understanding that, though small, it might contain qualities which would prove too difficult for me to imitate. I had to work it over and over again, for I could not get any shape in the thick, sticky paint. Then I tried a head by Van der Helst, and succeeded a little better.

At last I stopped before one of the heads in the "Syndics of the Cloth Merchants' Guild." The man in the left-hand corner, with the soft grey hair under the steeple-hat, had arrested my fancy. I felt that there was something in the portrait's beauty I could grasp and reproduce, though I saw at once that the technical treatment was entirely different from what I had attempted hitherto. However, the desire to reproduce this breadth of execution tempted me so much that I resolved to try my hand at it. I forget now what the copy looked like; I only remember that for years it hung on my studio wall.

So I tried to grasp the colour scheme, and the technique of the different artists, until the beauties of the so-called "Night Patrol" and the "Syndics" took such hold of me that nothing attracted me but what had come from the hand of the great master, the unique Rembrandt. In his work I found something which all the others lacked. Freedom and exuberance were his chief attractions, two qualities utterly barred and forbidden in the drawing class and in my teacher's studio.

Although Frans Hals impressed me more than any other painter with the power with which he wielded the brush, even he was put in the shade by Rembrandt's unsurpassable colour effects.

When I had looked at Rembrandt's pictures to my heart's content, I used to go down to the ground floor in the "Trippenhuis" to the print cabinet. Here I found his etchings beautifully arranged. It was a pleasant room overlooking a garden, and in the centre stood a long table covered with a green cloth, on which one could put down the portfolio and look at the gems they contained at leisure.

I often sat there for hours, buried in the contemplation of these two hundred and forty masterpieces. The conservator never ceased urging me to be careful when he saw me mix them up too much in my efforts to compare them. How astonished I was to find in the painter who, with mighty hand, had modelled in paint the glorious "Night Patrol," an accomplished engraver, not only gifted with the power and freedom of a great painter, but thoroughly versed in all the mysteries of the use of the etching needle on the hard, smooth copper.

Still it was not the extraordinary skill which attracted me most in these etchings. It was rather the singular inventive power shown in the different scenes, the peculiar contrast between light and shade, and the almost childlike manner in which the figures had been treated. The artist's soul not only spoke through the choice of subject, but it found an expression in every single detail, conveyed by the delicate handling of the needle.

Many Biblical subjects are represented in the Amsterdam collection; they are full of artistic imagination and sentiment in their composition in spite of their seeming incongruity. The conception is so highly original, and at the same time betrays such a depth of understanding, that other prints, however beautifully done, look academic and stilted beside them.

Among those etchings were excellent portraits, wonderfully lifelike heads of the painter's friends and of himself; but when one has looked at the little picture of his mother, he is compelled to shut the portfolio for a moment, because the unbidden tears rise to the eyes.

It is impossible to find anything more exquisite than this engraving. Motherly kindness, sweetness, and thoughtfulness are expressed in every curve, in the slightest touch of the needle. Each line has a meaning; not a single touch could have been left out without injury to the whole.

Hokusai, the Japanese artist, said that he hoped to live to be very old that he might have time to learn to draw in such a way that every stroke of his pencil would be the expression of some living thing. That is exactly what Rembrandt has attained here, and, in this portrait, he realised at the age of twenty-four the ideal of the old Japanese; it is one of his earliest etchings.

I re-open the portfolio to have a look at the pictures of the wonderful old Jewish beggars. They were types that were to be found by the score in the Amsterdam of those days, and Rembrandt delighted to draw them. One is almost inclined to say that they cannot be beggars, because the master's hand has endowed them with the warmth and splendour with which his artistic temperament clothed everything he looked at.

When I had looked enough at the etchings, I used to go home through the town, and it seemed to me as if I were meeting the very people I had just seen in the engravings. As I went through the "Hoog Straat" and "St. Anthony's Breestraat" to the "Joden Breestraat," where I lived a few doors from the famous house where Rembrandt dwelt and worked so long, I saw the picturesque crowd passing to and fro; I saw the vivid Hebrew physiognomies, with their iron-grey beards; the red-headed women; the barrows full of fish or fruit, or all kinds of rubbish; the houses, the people, the sky. It was all Rembrandt – all Rembrandtesque. A great deal has been changed in those streets since the time of which I have been writing, yet, even now, whenever I pass through them I seem to see the colours, and the kind of people Rembrandt shows us in his works.

In the meantime I had found a third manifestation of Rembrandt's talent, viz., his drawings. To a young painter, who himself was still groping in the dark for means of expressing his feelings, these drawings were exceedingly puzzling, but at the same time full of stimulus.

Less palpably living than his etchings, it was some time before I could properly appreciate them, but when I understood what I firmly believe still, namely, that the master did not draw with a view to exhibiting them or only for the pleasure of making graceful outlines I felt their true meaning. They were simply the embodiments of his deeper feelings; emanations from the abundance of his fertile imagination. They have been thrown on the paper with an unthinking, careless hand; the same hand that created masterpieces, prompted by the slightest impulse, the least sensation. When I looked at them superficially they seemed disfigured by all sorts of smudges and thick black lines, which cross and recross in a seemingly wild and aimless sort of way; but when looked into carefully, they all have a meaning of their own, and have been put there with a just and deep felt appreciation of light and shade. The greater compositions crowded with figures, the buildings, the landscapes – all are impregnated with the same deep artistic feeling.

One evening one of my friends gave us a short lecture on art and showed us many drawings by ancient and modern artists, most of them, however, being by contemporaries who had already become famous. Among them was one drawing by Rembrandt, and it was remarkable to notice the peculiar effect it produced in this collection. The scene represented on the old smudgy piece of paper was so simple in execution, so noble in composition, done with just a few strokes of the pencil, that all the other drawings looked like apprentice-work beside it. Here was the master, towering above all.

Thus I saw Rembrandt, the man who could tell me endless stories, and could conjure them up before my eyes with either brush, pencil, or etching needle. Whether heaven or earth; the heroes of old; or only a corner of old Amsterdam – out of everything he made the most beautiful drawings. His pictures of lions and elephants are wonderfully naïve. His nude figures of female models are remarkable, because no painter dared paint them exactly as he saw them in his studio, but Rembrandt, entranced by the glow and warmth of the flesh tints, never dreamt of reproducing them otherwise than as he saw them. It was no Venus, or June, or Diana he wanted. He might, perhaps, even take his neighbour's washerwoman, make her get up on the model throne, and put her on the canvas in all the glory of living, throbbing flesh and blood.

And the way in which he put his scrawls and strokes is so wonderful that one can never look too long at them. All his work is done with a light-heartedness, a cheerfulness, and firmness which preclude at once the idea of painful study and exertion.

☆ 32

II

What do I think of the master now, after so many years?

Come with me, reader, let us look together at the strongest expression of Rembrandt's art, viz., his picture "The Night Patrol."

Our way leads us now to the Ryksmuseum, and we sit down in the newly built "Rembrandt room," with our backs to the light, so as to obtain a full view of the picture, and we try to forget all about the struggle it cost to erect this temple of art.

At first sight, we are struck by the grand movements of light and shade, which seem to flood the canvas as if with waves of coloured harmonies. Then, suddenly, two men seem to step out from the group. The one is dressed in sombre-coloured clothes, whilst the other is resplendent in white. That is Rembrandt all over, not afraid of putting the light in bold contrast against the dark. So as to maintain the harmony between the two he makes the dark man lift his hand as if he were pointing at something, and in doing so, he casts a softening shadow on his brilliant companion. Genius finds a way where ordinary mortals are at a loss how to help themselves. Clearly these men are in earnest conversation with each other, and it is quite evident that they are the leaders of the company.

But when everything was put on the canvas that he intended to put there, the master stood in front of it and shook his head.

☆ 34

To him these two leaders did not stand out sufficiently from the rest. So he took up his palette again, and again he dipped his broadest brushes deep in paint and with a few mighty strokes he transformed these two figures; a little more depth here, some more light there. He tried every means to give the scene more depth, and a fuller meaning. Then he saw that it was all right and left it.

The likeness of his patrons was, perhaps, not very exact and most likely some murmurs were raised at the want of minutely finished detail; but he did not heed such matters. To him the main point was to make his figures live and breathe and move; and see how he succeeded! From the plumes of their hats to the soles of their feet everything is living, tangible. How full of energy and character are their heads! Their dress, the steel gorget, the boots of the man in white; everything bears witness to the wonderful power of the master.

And look at the man in black, with his red bandolier, his gloves, and his stick. This does not strike one as anything out of the common, because the composition is so true, so perfectly natural and simple. I cannot remember having seen a single picture in which the peculiar style and picturesqueness of those days is so vividly expressed, as in the figures of these two men calmly walking along on the giant canvas.

Now let us turn to the right and have a look at the perspiring drummer. His pock-marked face, overshadowed by a frayed hat, is of the true Falstaff type. The swollen nose, the thick-lipped mouth, every detail is carried out with the daring of the true artist which characterises all the master's work. Look at him, drumming away as if he wanted to make it known that he himself is one of the most magnificent specimens of the work of the genius whom men call Rembrandt.

On looking at this man I can understand why Gerard de Lairesse exclaimed in his great book on painting: "In Rembrandt's pictures the paint is running down the panel like mud!" But it was only his conscientious narrow-mindedness which made him say it. Genius never fails to get into conflict with narrow thought.

But now let us turn our attention to the left-hand corner. There we see that pithy soldier all in red. Rembrandt, with his intuitive knowledge of chiaroscuro, was not afraid of painting a figure all in red. He knew that the play of light and shade on the colour would help him out. Here part of the red is toned down by a beautiful soft tint, which makes the whole figure blend harmoniously with the greyish-green of the others. This man in red, too, has been treated in the same masterly manner of which I spoke above. If one looks at him attentively, it seems as if the man, who apparently might step out of the canvas at any rate, had been painted with one powerful sweep of the brush. How firm is the treatment of the hand loading the gun; how true the shadows on the red hat and jerkin. There the figure stands, alert, living, full of movement, rich in colour.

In this marvellous picture we come across something striking at every turn. How life-like is the halberdier looking over his shoulder; and the man who is inspecting his gun, just behind the figure in white; observe the wonderful effect of the laughing boy in the grey hat against the dark background. Even the pillar which serves as a background to the man with the helmet adds to the harmony of the whole.

But here we meet with something peculiar! What is that quaint little girl doing among all those men?

Numbers of critics have racked their brains about the meaning of different details. But if Rembrandt could have heard them, he would have answered with a laugh, "Don't you see that I only wanted this child as a focus for the light, and a contrast with all the downward lines and dark colours?"

The man with the banner in the background, the dog running away, all these details help each other to carry out the effect of line and colour. There is not a square inch in this canvas which does not betray a rare talent. This is a case in which the assertion, "Cut me a piece out of a picture and I will tell you if it is by an artist," could successfully be applied.

Now, I hope my readers won't object to accompanying me a little further, and stopping with me before the "Syndics." There it hangs, the great simple canvas, quite different in character from the "Night Patrol."

Everything here is dignified and stately. The whole picture is a glorious witness to the consummate knowledge the master possessed of expressing the individual soul in the human face. Here they sit, those old Dutch fathers, assembled in solemn conclave, debating about their trade, with the books on the table in front of them; and Rembrandt has painted these heads so true to life that in the course of years they have become like old friends; yes, old friends, though they lived hundreds of years before we were dreamt of.

How long have I known that man on the left, with his hand on the knob of his arm-chair, and the fine grey hair on his broad wrinkled brow showing from under the high steeple-hat? The flesh tints in the face, whether catching the full light, or partly veiled by shadows, display an endless variety of shades, and the neutral greens and reds, greys and yellows, are put against each other in such a wonderful manner that an effect has been attained which strikes us dumb with admiration. The way in which he is made to stand out from the background is in itself marvellous, but just look at the man! how full of life and understanding is the look in those eyes. It is something quite unique, something Rembrandt himself has never surpassed.

And then there are the other figures; the man who is leaning forward; the one sitting right in front of the book, his neighbour; even the fifth merchant on the right, with his servant behind him – one and all are full of life and light.

The background is such as Rembrandt only, with his understanding of lines, could have devised. The wall and the panelling shut in the composition in such a way that one cannot possibly imagine it ever having been otherwise. And even this skilful touch is made subordinate to the warm red colour of the tablecloth, which lends the picture an additional depth.

I don't know whether this picture was very much discussed by Rembrandt's contemporaries when it was finished. But to us, who have seen so much of the art of the great Italians, Germans, and Spaniards, these heads are the highest achievement of the art of painting.

When I was in Madrid, where I was charmed by Velasquez' work, our party was one day walking through the broad streets of the capital. Passing a large, picturesque building, our attention was attracted by a gaudy poster informing us that an exhibition of the works of modern Spanish artists was being held within. Our curiosity being aroused, we entered, and found that in this country, where so many famous artists lived and worked, there are among the modern artists many studious, highly talented men, who serve their art with true love and devotion. But suddenly it seemed as if we had been carried by magic from Spain back to Amsterdam. We had come face to face with a copy of the "Syndics," painted by a Spanish artist during a stay in Amsterdam.

Was it national prejudice, or was it conviction? I don't know; but this copy spoke to us of a spirit of greater simplicity, of a truer conception of the nature and dignity of mankind than anything we had admired in the Prado. Yes; this picture even kills its own Dutch brothers. It makes Van der Helst look superficial, and Franz Hals unfinished and flat. So much thoroughness and depth combined with such freedom and grace of movement is not to be found anywhere else.

These people have lived on the canvas for centuries, and they will outlive us all. And the man who achieved this masterpiece was at the time of its production a poor, struggling burgher living in an obscure corner of the town where his tercentenary festival was lately celebrated.

III

But this is not the place for the sad reflections which are awakened in our minds on examining the records of him whose name the world now glorifies and raises to the skies. Better to honour the great master who, for so many centuries, has held the world in awed admiration. There is no need to-day to drag Rembrandt forth from the obscurity of the past to save him from oblivion; we were not obliged to cleanse his image from the dust of ages before showing to the world this unequalled genius to whom Holland proudly points as one of her own sons.

On the contrary, never was Rembrandt's art valued so highly as it is now. Archives and documents are searched for details about his life and works. We want to know all about his life, and are anxious to share his inmost feelings in prosperity and adversity. The houses where he lived are marked down and bought by art-lovers. At the present time Rembrandt is in the zenith of his glory. Gold loses its value where his pictures are concerned. Fortunes are spent to secure the most insignificant of his works; people travel across continents to see them; and criticism, which for long years did little more than snarl at Rembrandt, has for nearly fifty years been dumb.

It is remarkable that none of the great painters have, in the course of years, been subjected to so much criticism as Rembrandt. And notwithstanding all the things which have been said about the improbability of the scene, and the exaggeration of the dark background, the "Night Patrol" is now, as it ever was and ever will be, the "World's wonder," as our English neighbours say.

During his lifetime there were people who condemned Rembrandt because he refused to follow in the footsteps of the old Italian painters, because he persisted in painting nature as he saw it.

To us such a reproach seems strange, yet it is quite true. Even during the last years of Rembrandt's life a growing dissatisfaction with the existing ideas on art and literature had taken possession of the Dutch mind. People developed a morbid taste for everything classical; and when I read in the prose works and poems of these days the Latinised names and the constant allusions to Greek gods and goddesses and mythological personages, so strangely out of place under our northern sky, I am filled with disgust.

It was fortunate, indeed, that Rembrandt always felt strong in his own conviction and only followed his own views. For many years after his death, even as late as the middle of the nineteenth century, a number of art critics raised objections against the dangerous theories of which his pictures were the expression. Again and again they attacked his technical treatment; none of them ever grasped its deeper, fuller meaning.

Happily those days are far behind us. A great number of books and pamphlets have been published on Rembrandt during the last fifty years, and they are almost unanimous in their praise and admiration of the great master. The more liberal feelings of the modern world have achieved some victories in the realms of art as well as elsewhere. We moderns feel that the apparent shortcomings and exaggerations are nothing but the inevitable peculiarities attendant upon genius. And we even go so far that we would not have him be without a single one of them, for fear of losing the slightest trait in the character of the great man whose every movement roused our intellectual faculties.

So Rembrandt has been raised in our days to the pinnacle of

fame which is his by right; the festival of his tercentenary was acknowledged by the whole civilised world as the natural utterance of joy and pride of our small country in being able to count among its children the great Rembrandt.

I finish, – "with the pen, but not with the heart!" For if I should go on until the inclination to add more to what I have written here should fail me, my readers would have tired of me long before I had tired of my subject. I am thinking of that rare gem, the portrait of Jan Six – of the Louvre, of Cassel, of Brunswick, of what not!

May these pages convey to the reader the fact that I have always looked upon Rembrandt as the true type of an artist, free, untrammelled by traditions, genial in all he did; in short, a figure in whom all the great qualities of the old Republic of the United Provinces were concentrated and reflected.

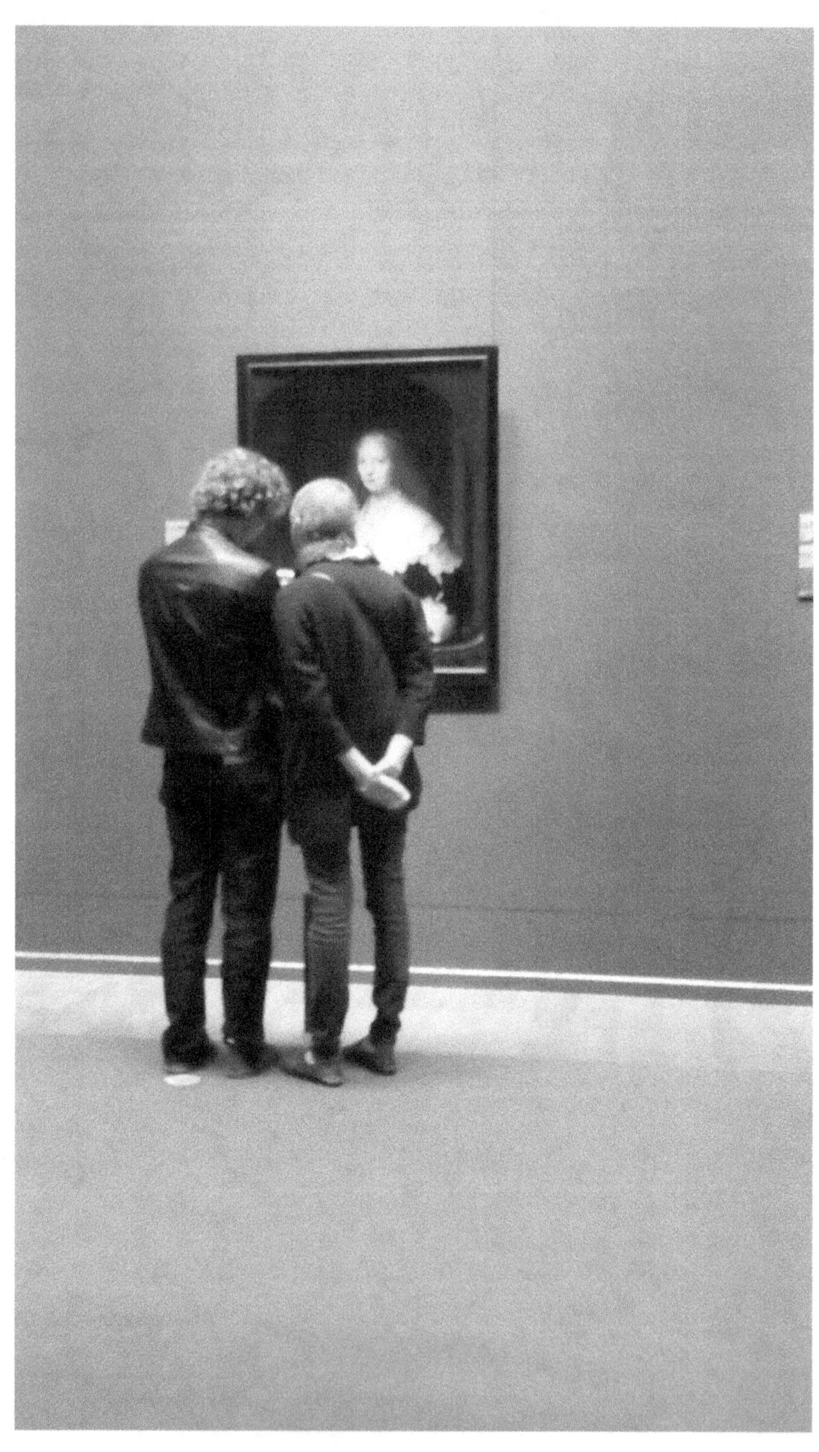

Rembrandt in the Rijksmusem, Amsterdam, 2015
(this page and over. Photos: J. Robinson).

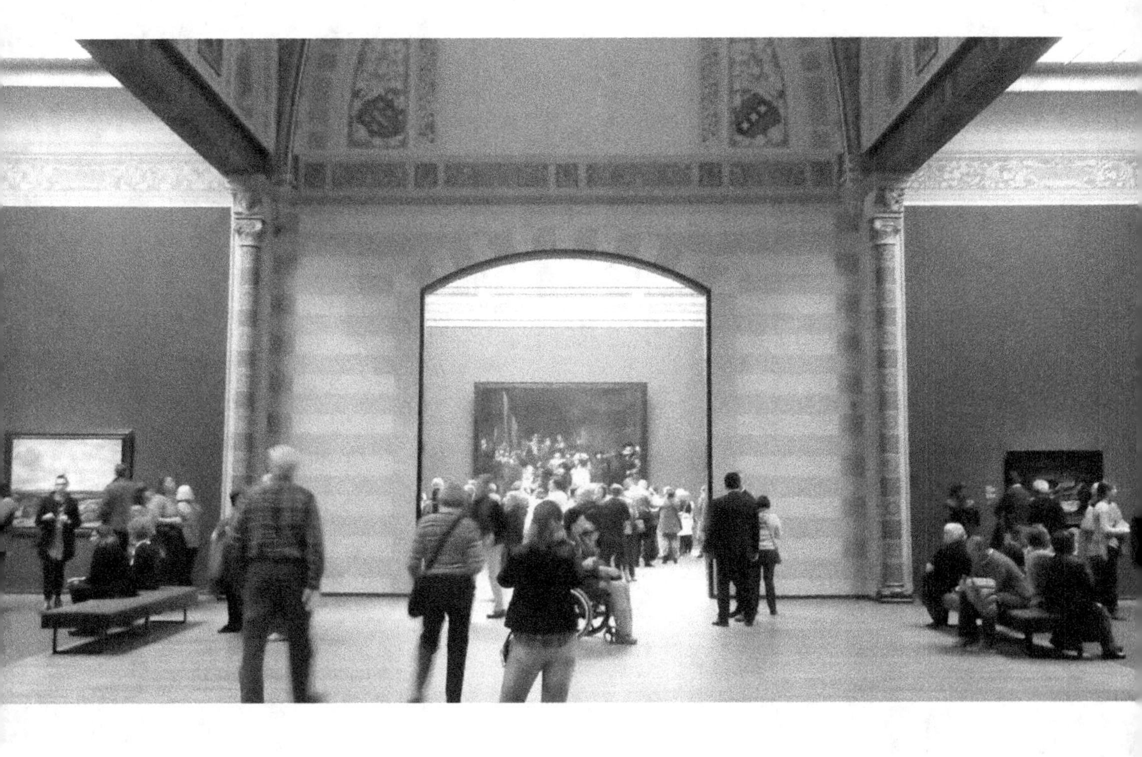

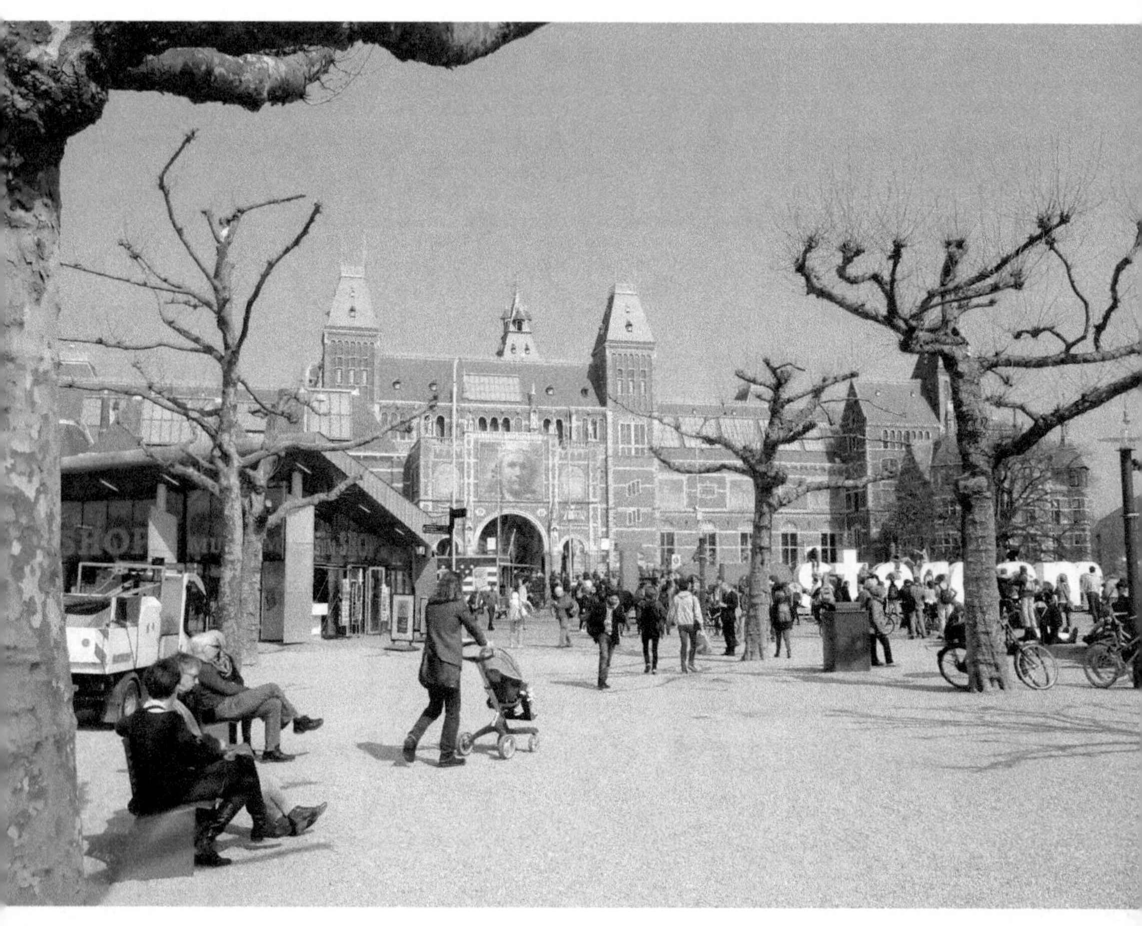

The Rijksmuseum in Amsterdam

Rembrandt, Self-Portrait, 1640, London
(this page and over)

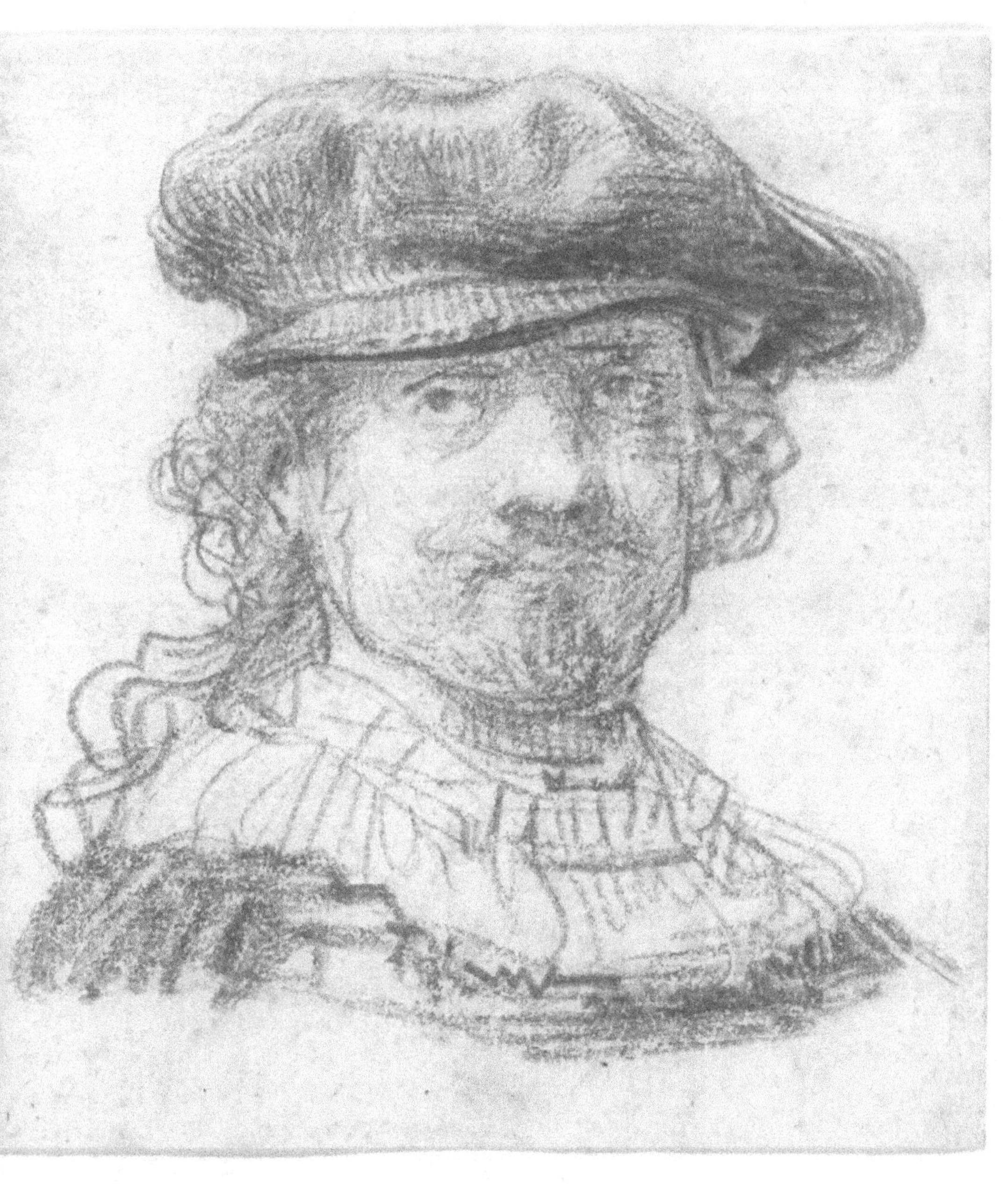

Rembrandt van Rijn, Self-Portrait, c.1637, Washington, DC

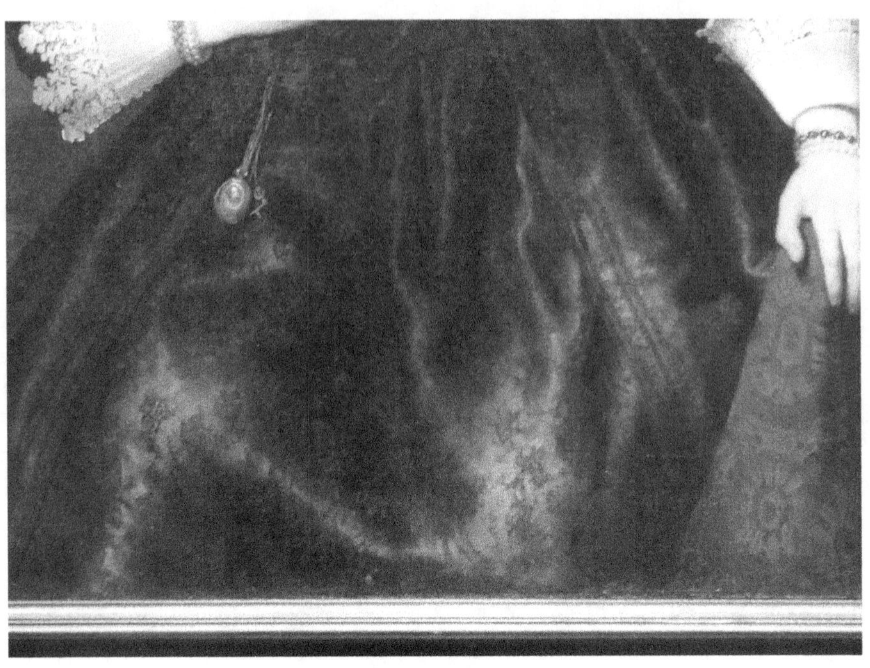

Rembrandt, Portrait of a Young Woman, details

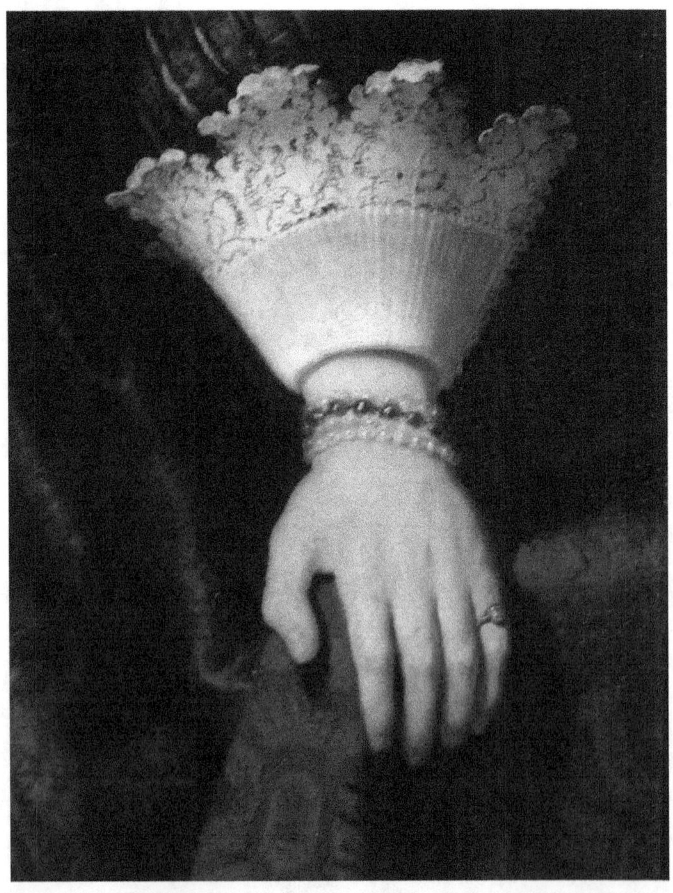

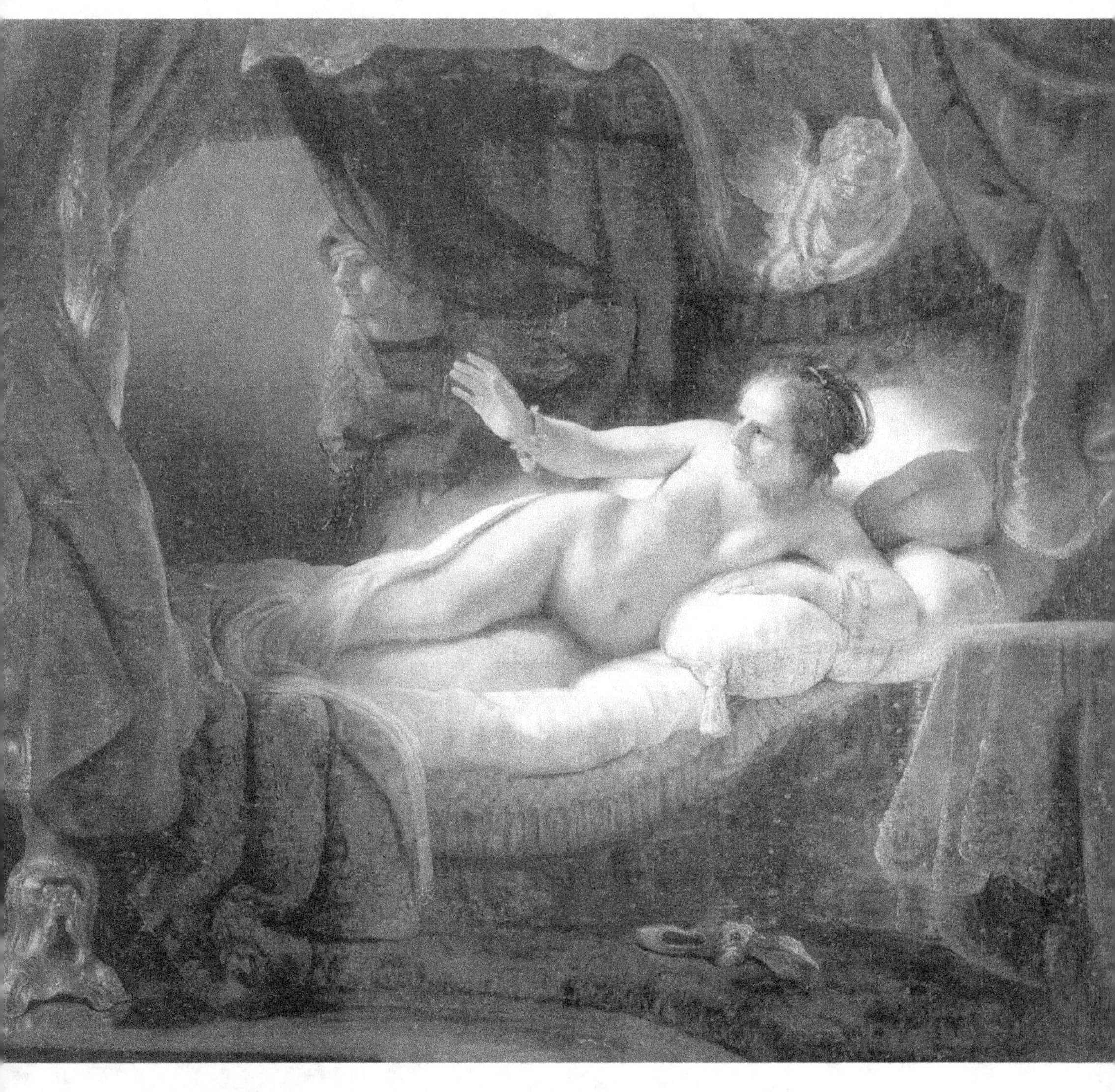

Rembrandt van Rijn, Danae, 1636, St Petersburg

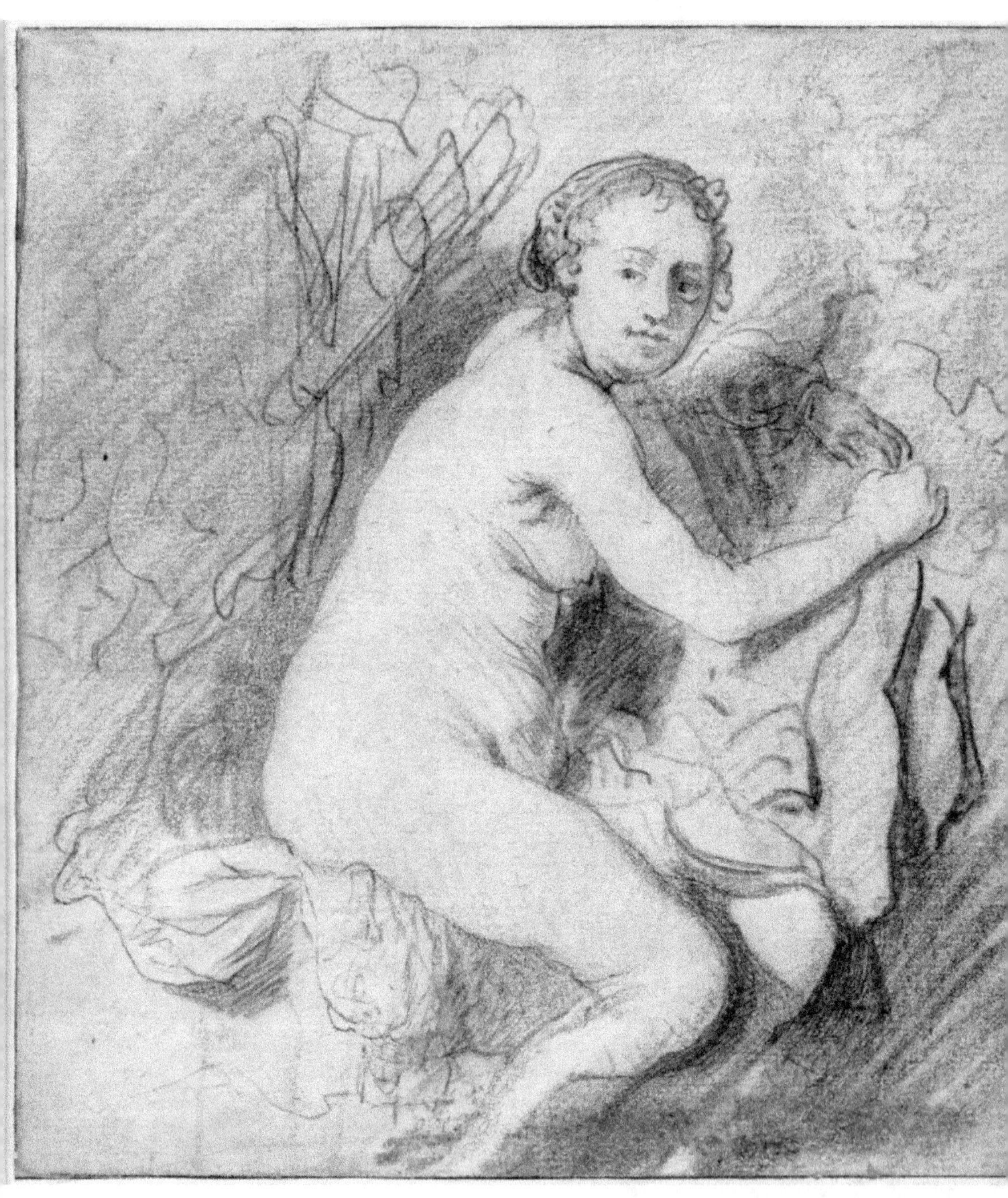

Rembrandt van Rijn, Diana At the Bath, 1630-31, British Museum

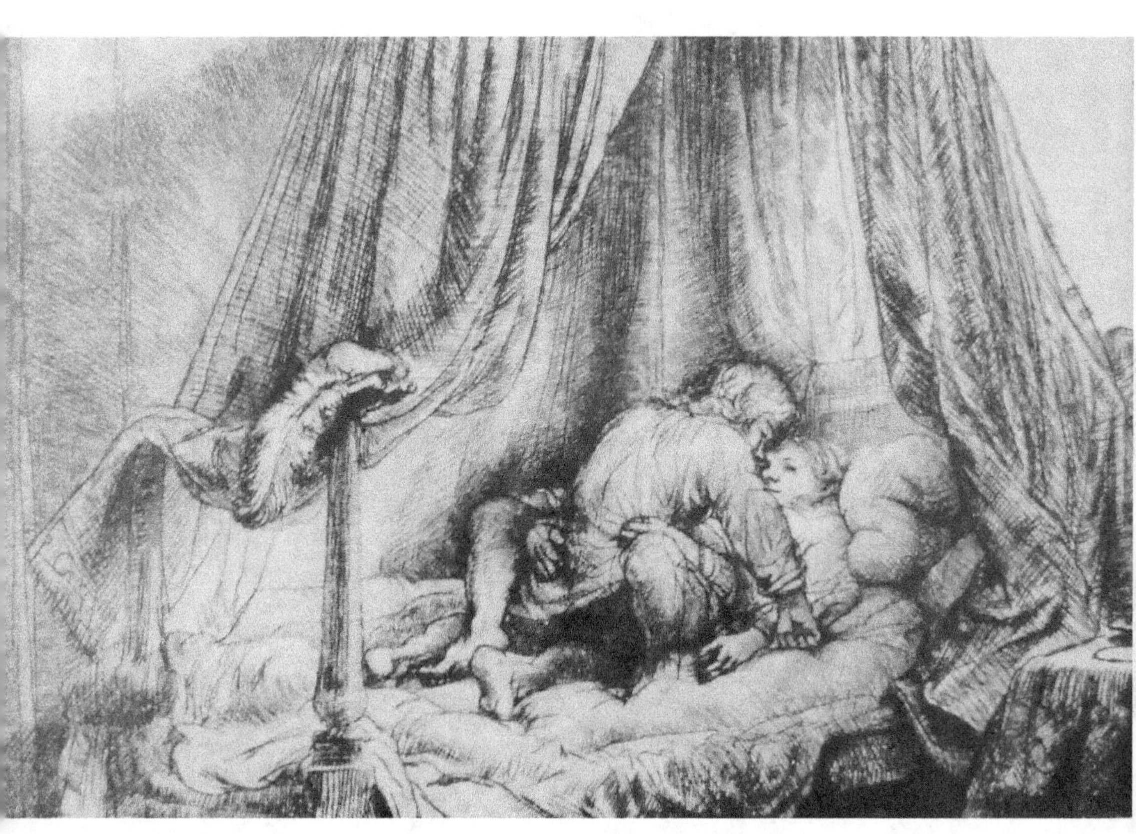

Rembrandt van Rijn, Ledakant, 1646

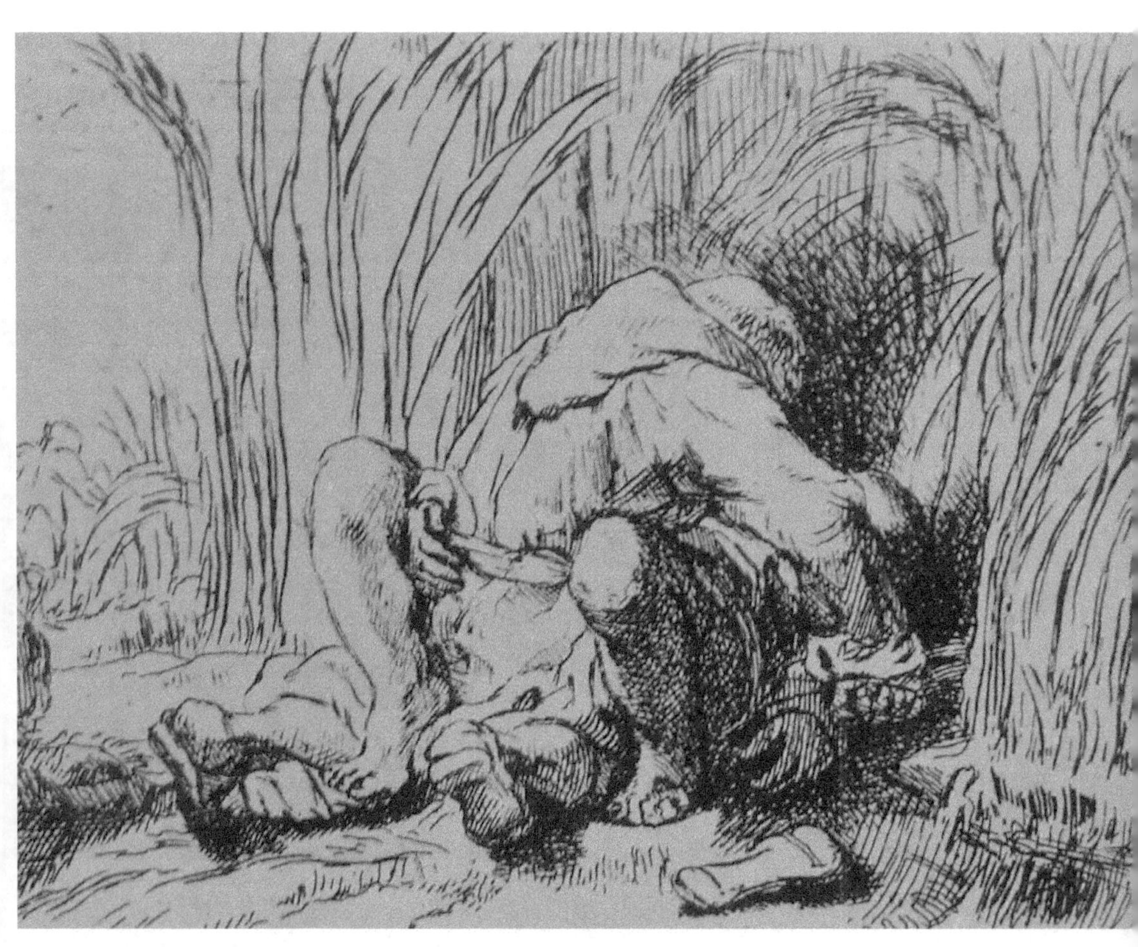

Rembrandt van Rijn, The Monk In the Cornfield

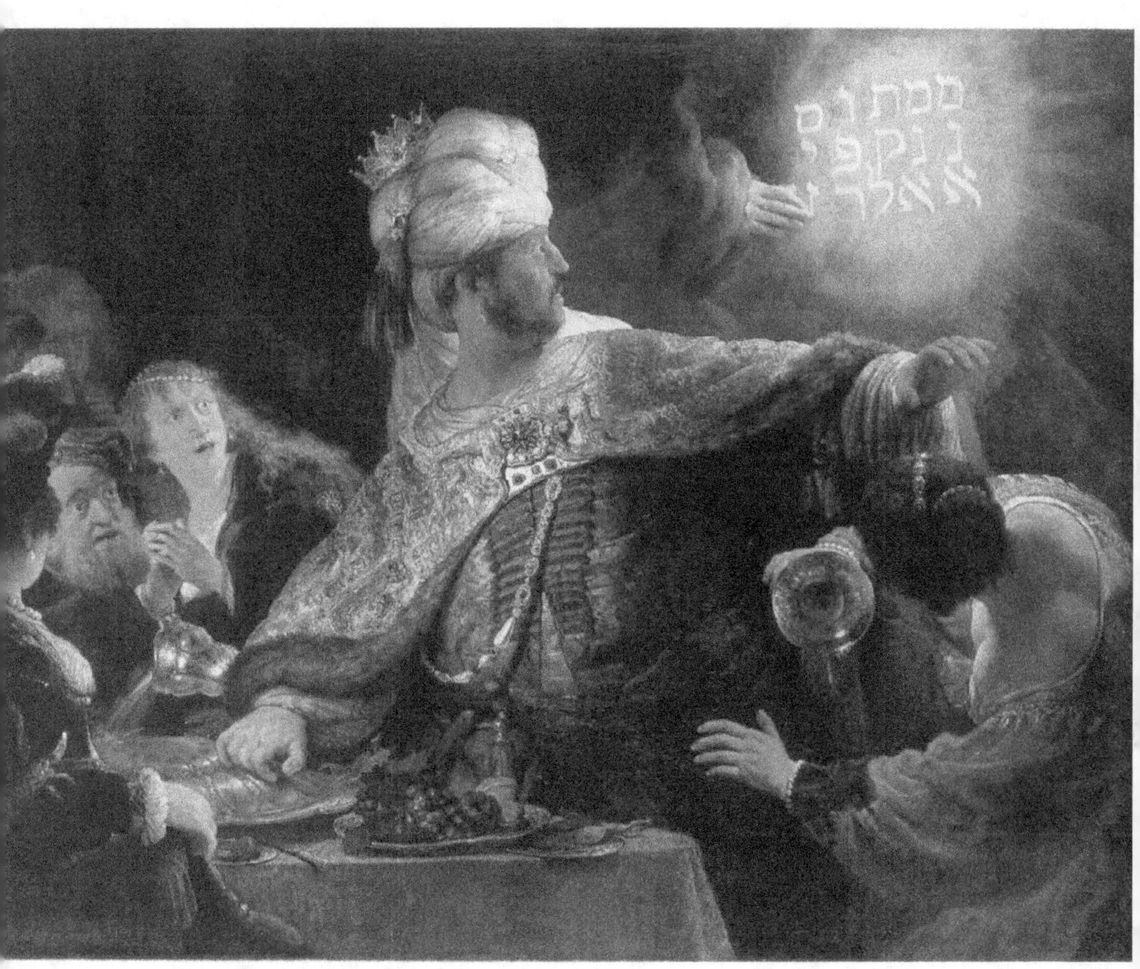

Rembrandt van Rijn, Belshazzar's Feast, 1635, National Gallery, London

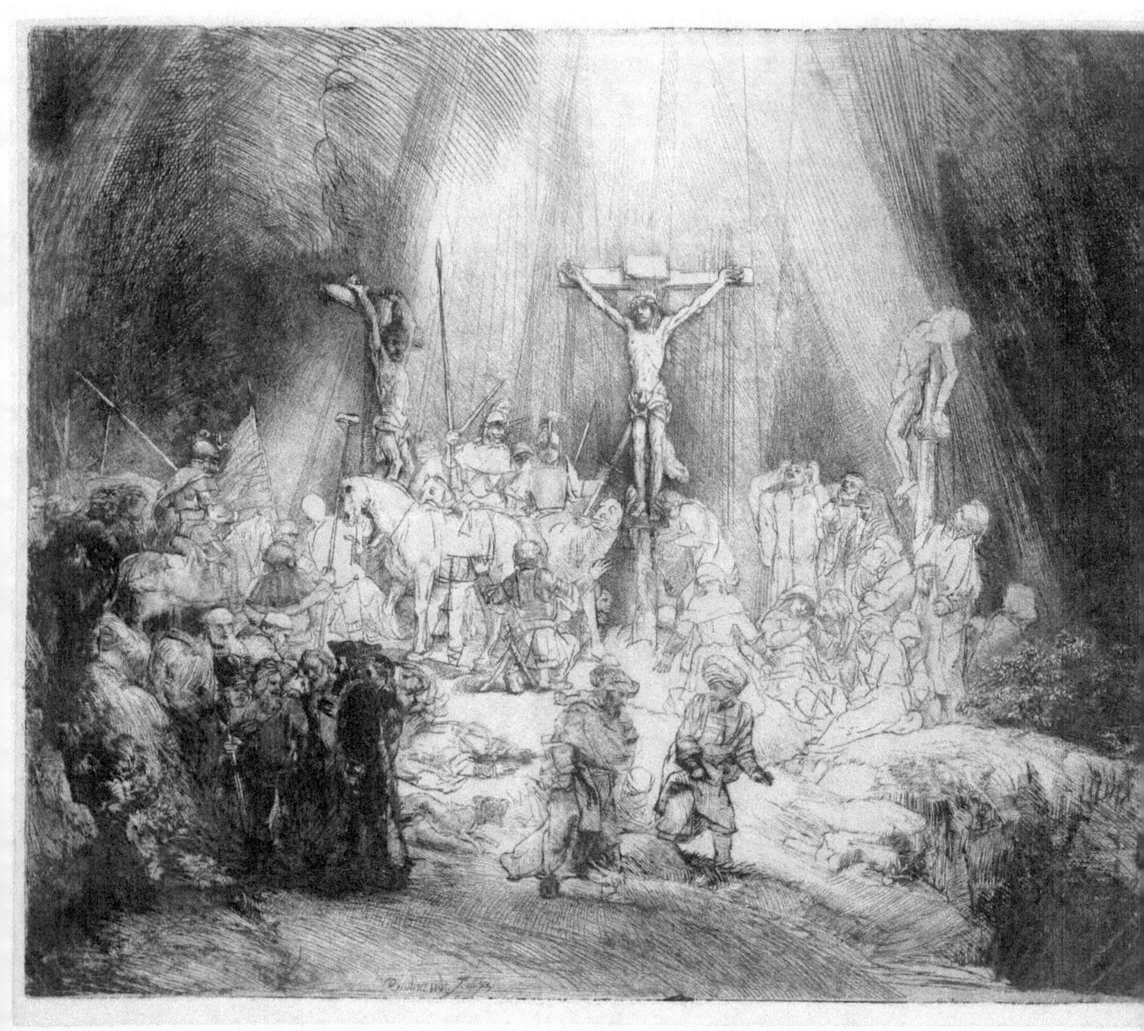

Rembrandt, The Three Crosses, 1653

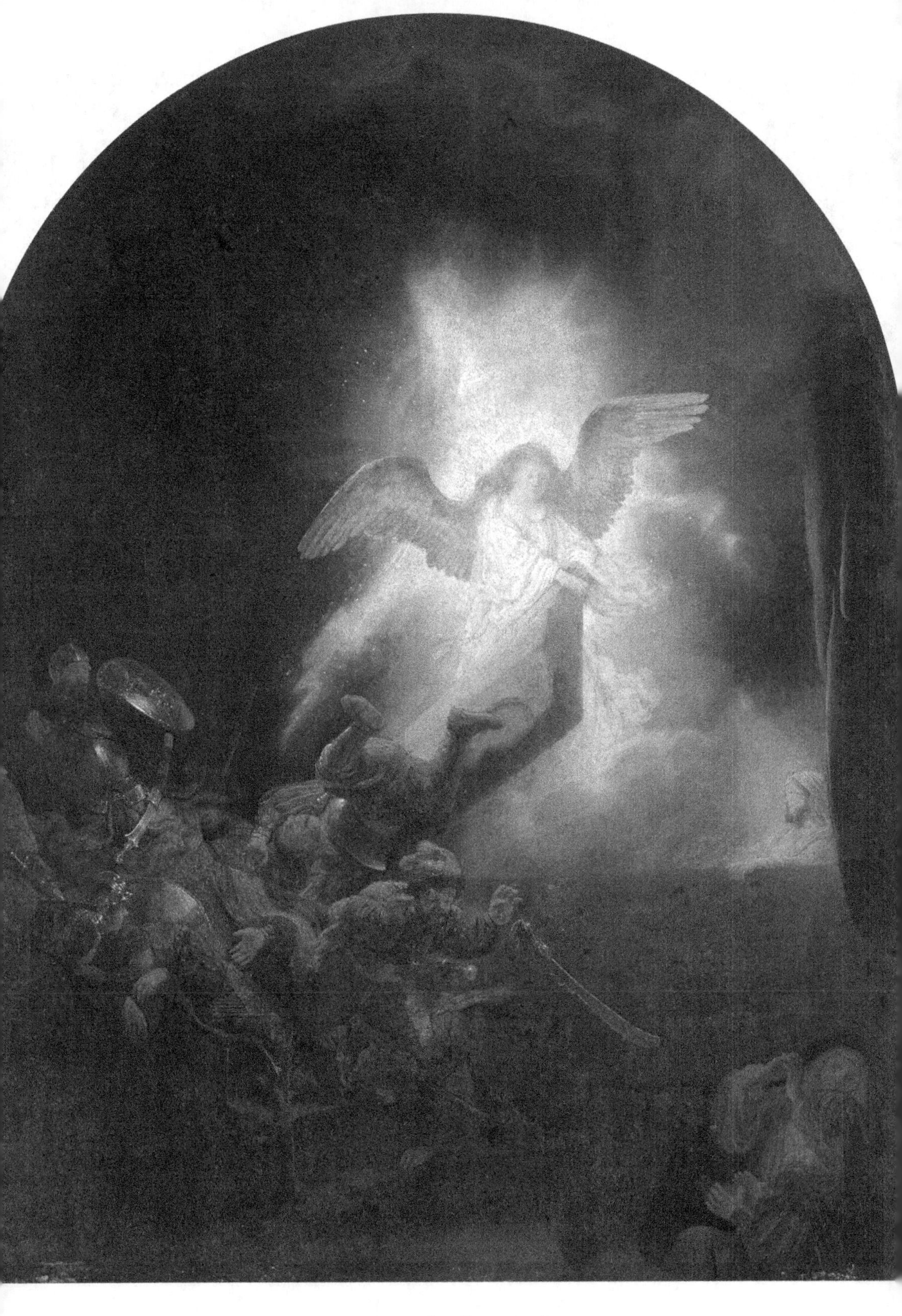

Rembrandt, The Resurrection

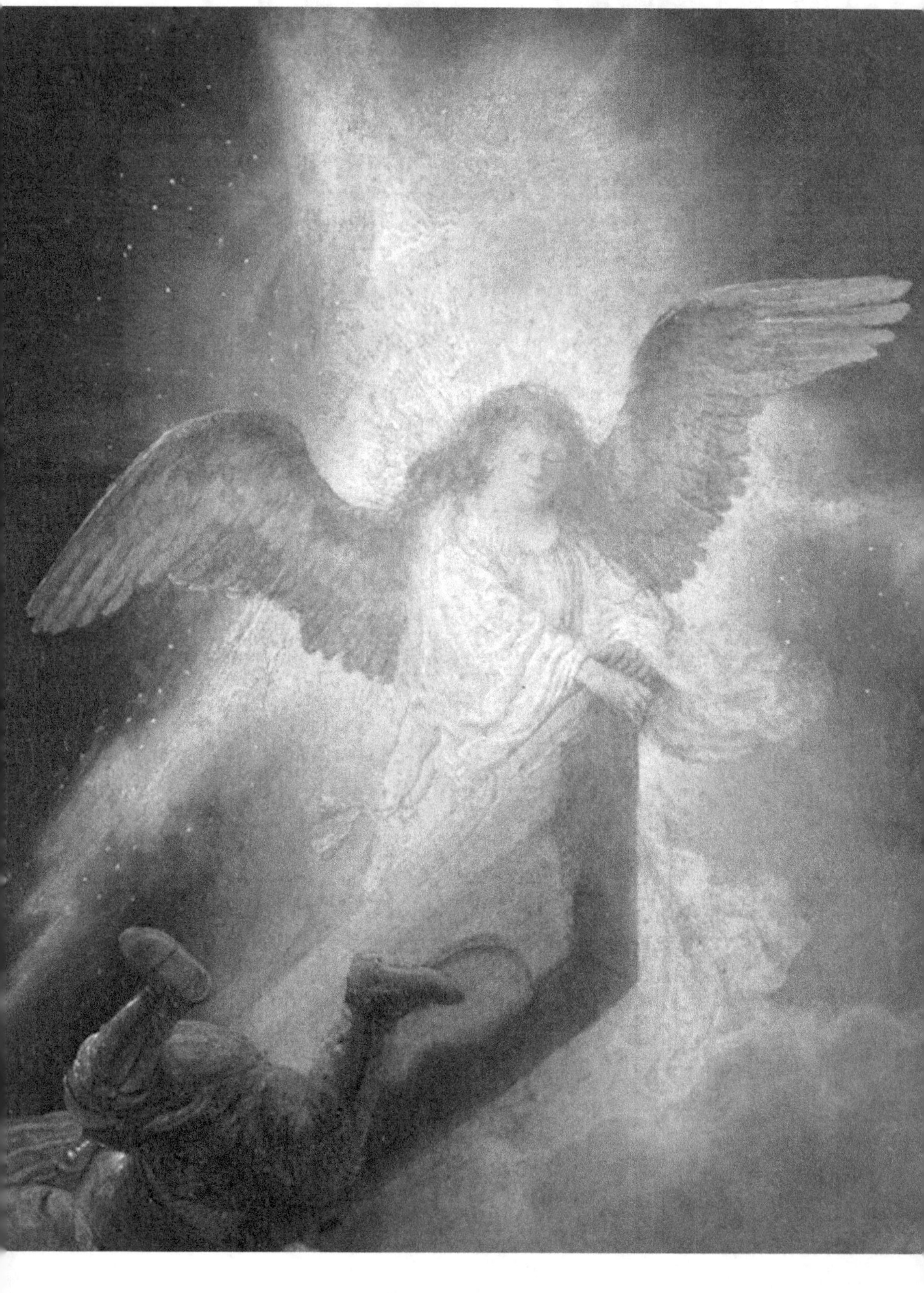

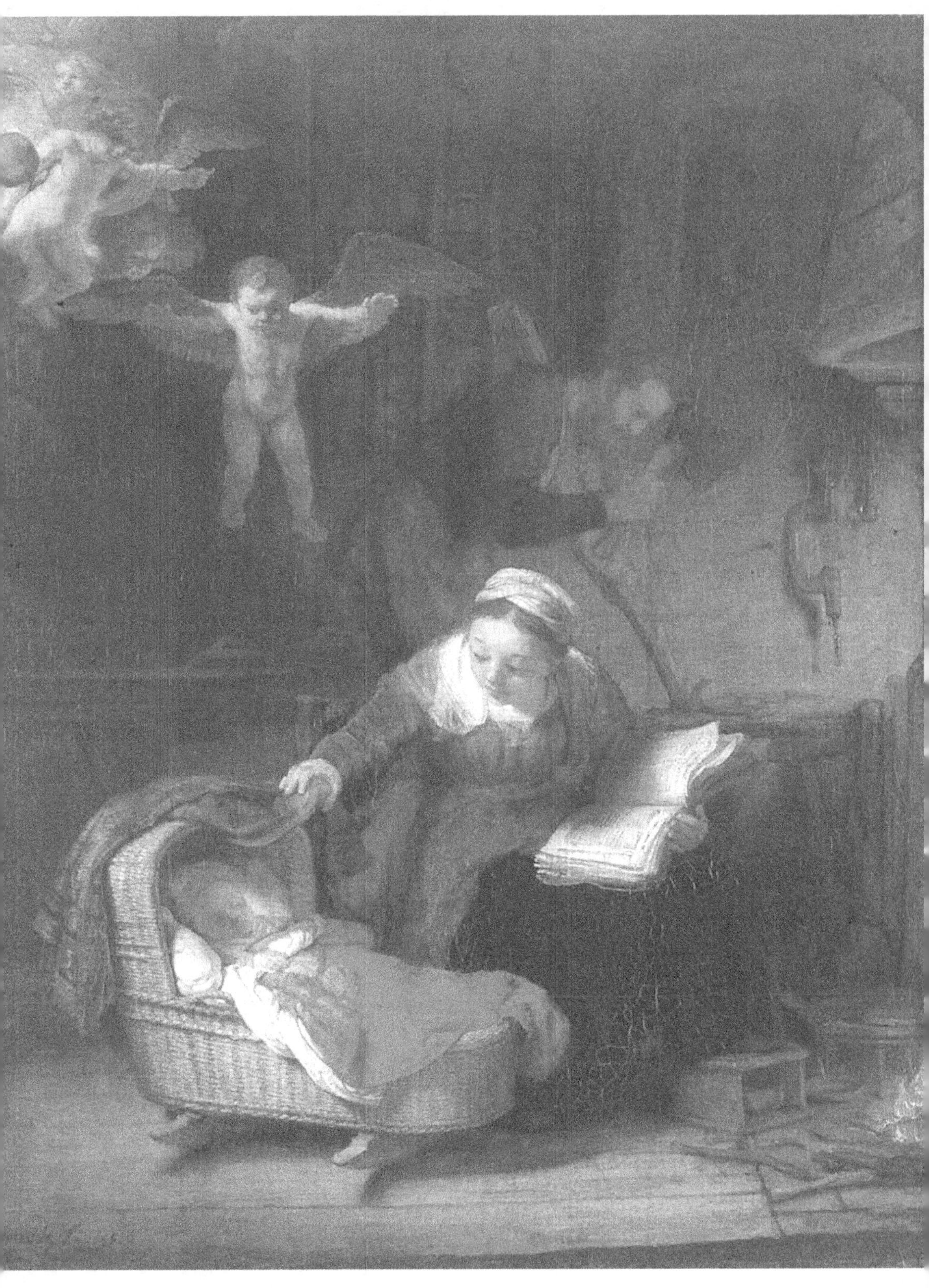

Rembrandt van Rijn, The Holy Family With Angels, 1645, Hermitage Museum

NOTES ON WORKS

SUZANNA VAN COLLEN

This portrait, painted about 1633, and one of the gems of the Wallace Collection, presents Susanna van Collen, wife of Jan Pellicorne, and her daughter.

A PORTRAIT OF SASKIA

Rembrandt's portraits of his wife Saskia are distributed fairly equally throughout the world's great galleries, but this one from the Brera in Milan is not so well known as most, and on this account it is reproduced here. It is called "Portrait of a Woman" in the catalogue, but the features justify the belief that the lady was the painter's wife.

SYNDICS OF THE CLOTH MERCHANTS' GUILD

This fine work, of which so much has been written, is to be

seen to-day in the Royal Museum at Amsterdam. It is one of the finest examples of the master's portrait groups, and was painted in 1661.

PORTRAIT OF AN OLD MAN

Rembrandt painted very many portraits of men and women whose identity cannot be traced, and it is probable that the original of this striking portrait in the Pitti Palace at Florence was unknown to many of the painter's contemporaries. This is one of Rembrandt's late works, and is said to have been painted about 1658.

THE COMPANY OF FRANCIS BANNING COCQ

Generally known as the "Night Watch." This famous picture, now to be seen in the Royal Museum at Amsterdam, is the best discussed of all the master's works. It has been pointed out that it is in reality a day scene although it is known to most people as the "Night Watch." The picture was painted in 1642.

PORTRAIT OF A YOUNG MAN

This portrait may be seen to-day in the Pitti Palace at Florence. It is said to be one of Rembrandt's portraits of himself, painted about 1635.

PORTRAIT OF AN OLD LADY

This famous portrait of an old lady unknown is in our
National Gallery. It is on canvas 4 ft. 2? in. by 3 ft. 2 in.

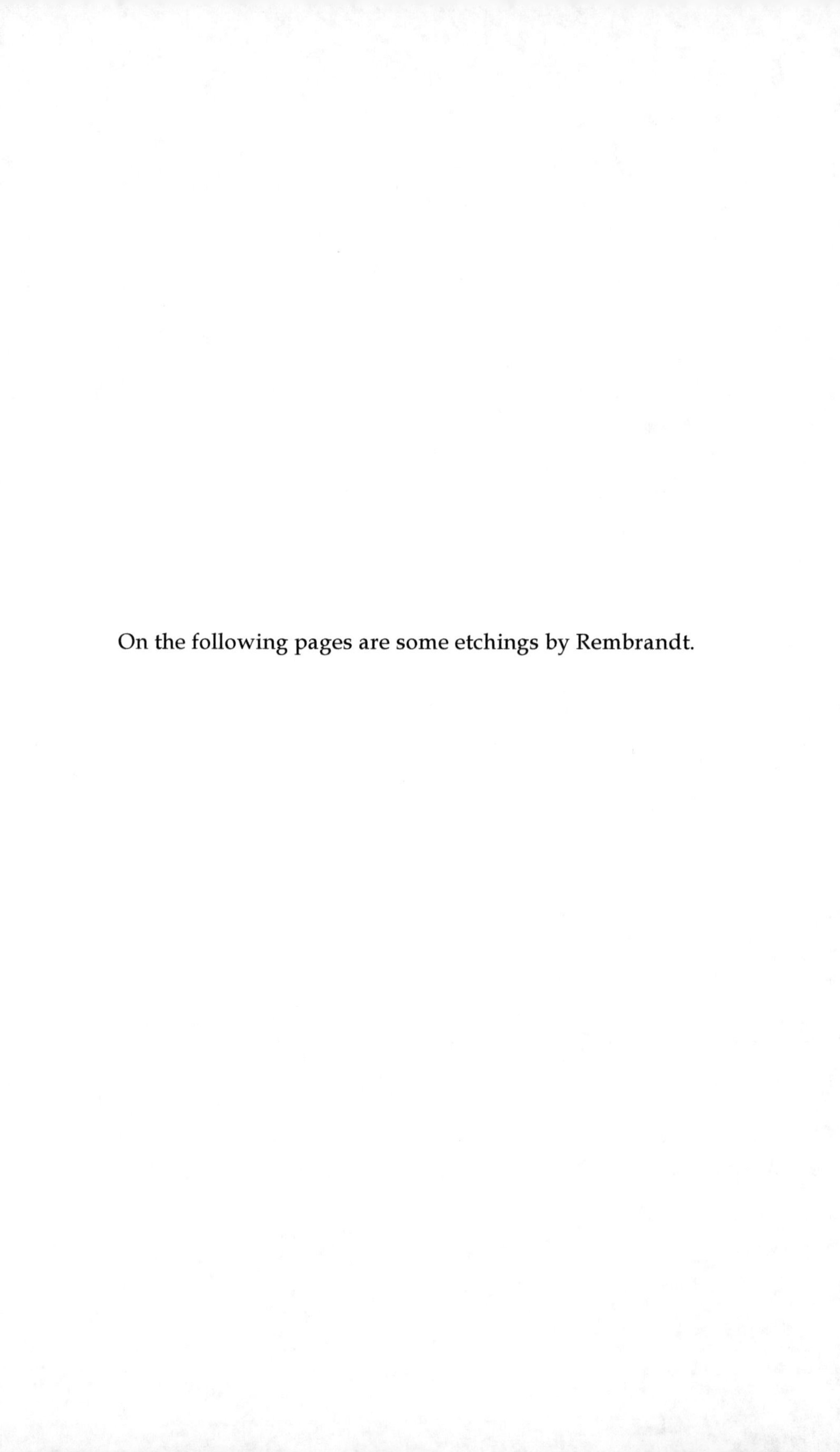

On the following pages are some etchings by Rembrandt.

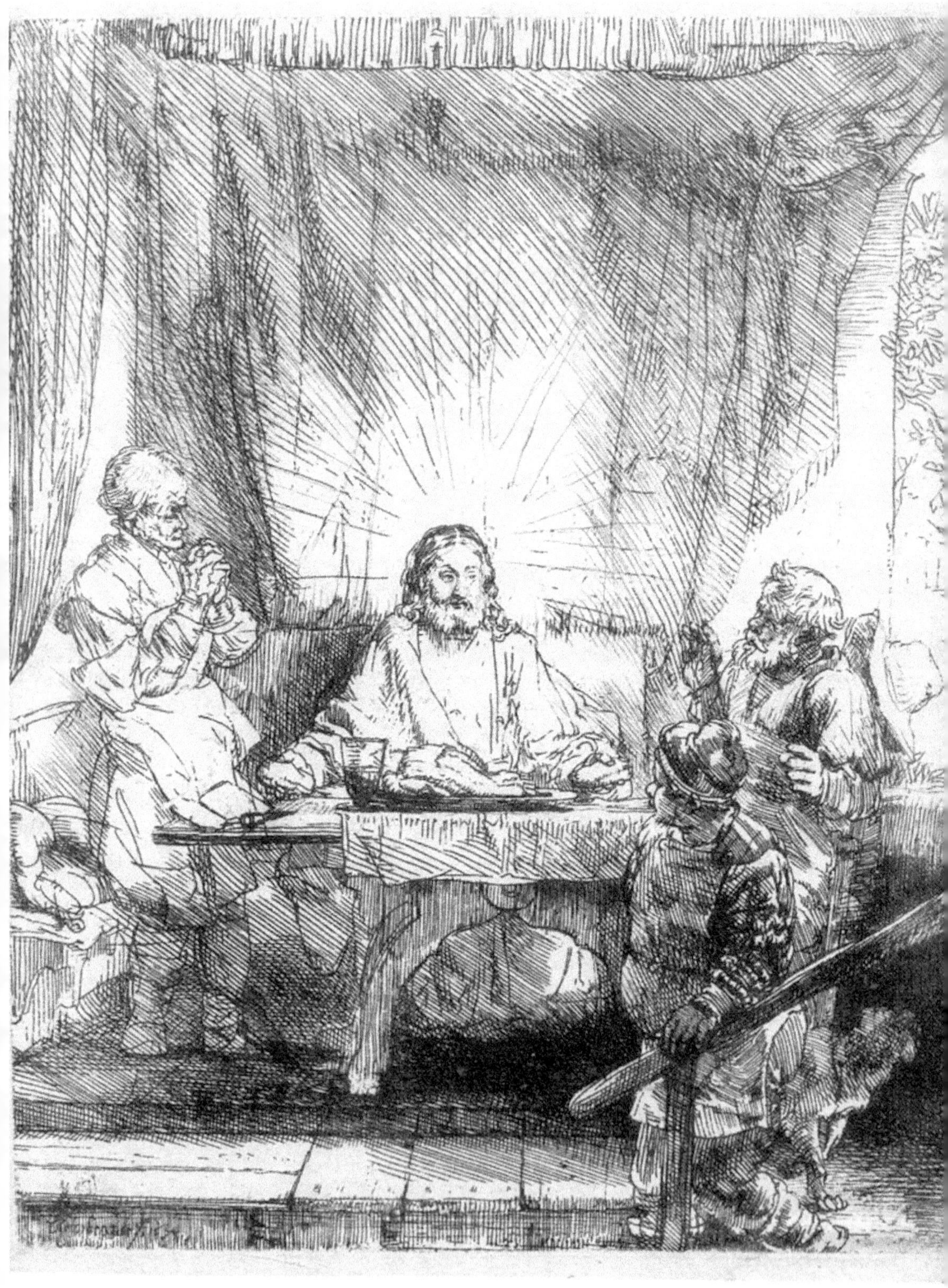

Rembrandt, Christ At Emmaus, 1654

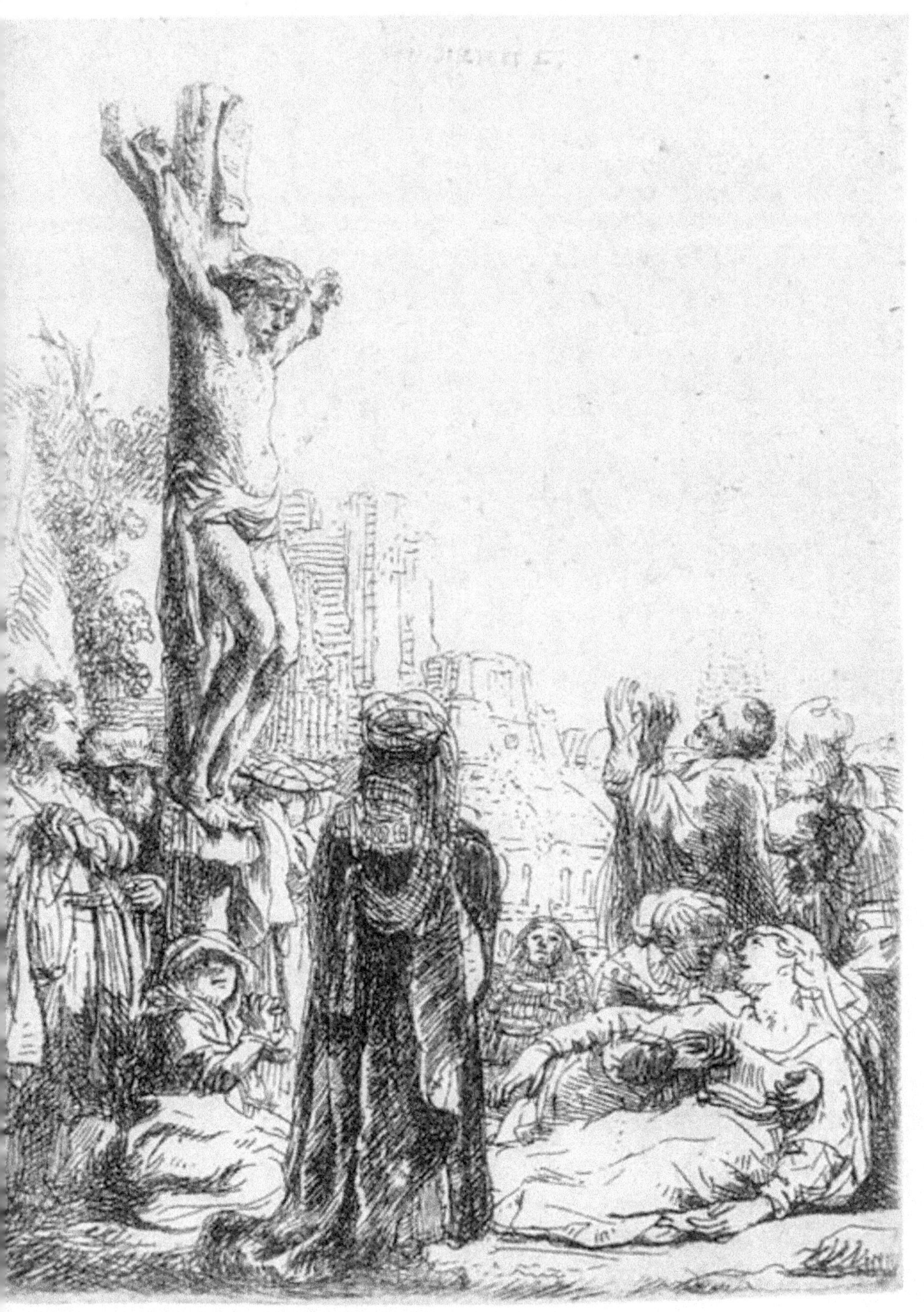

Rembrandt, The Crucifixion, 1637, Vienna

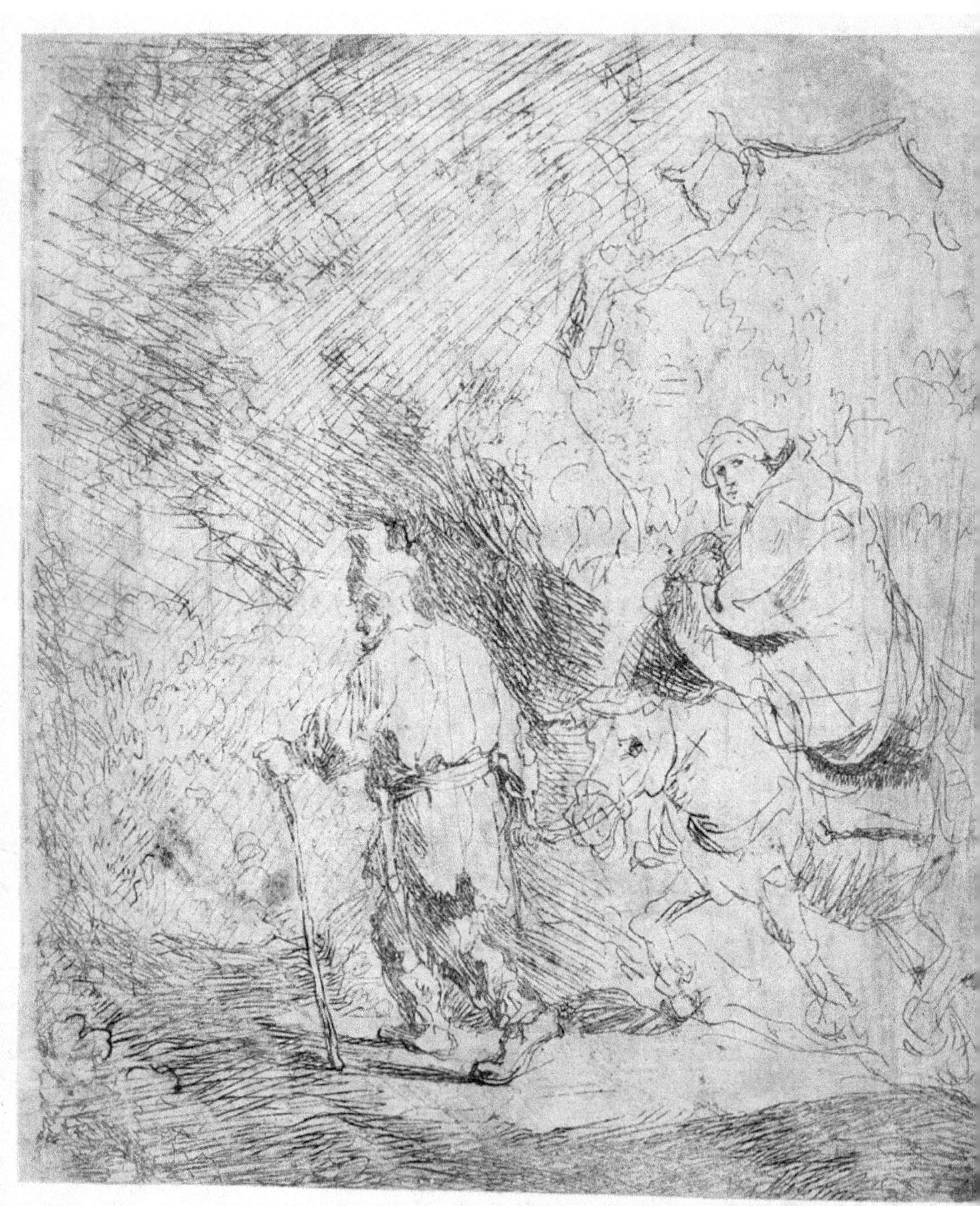

Rembrandt, The Flight Into Egypt, 1627, Rijksmuseum, Amsterdam

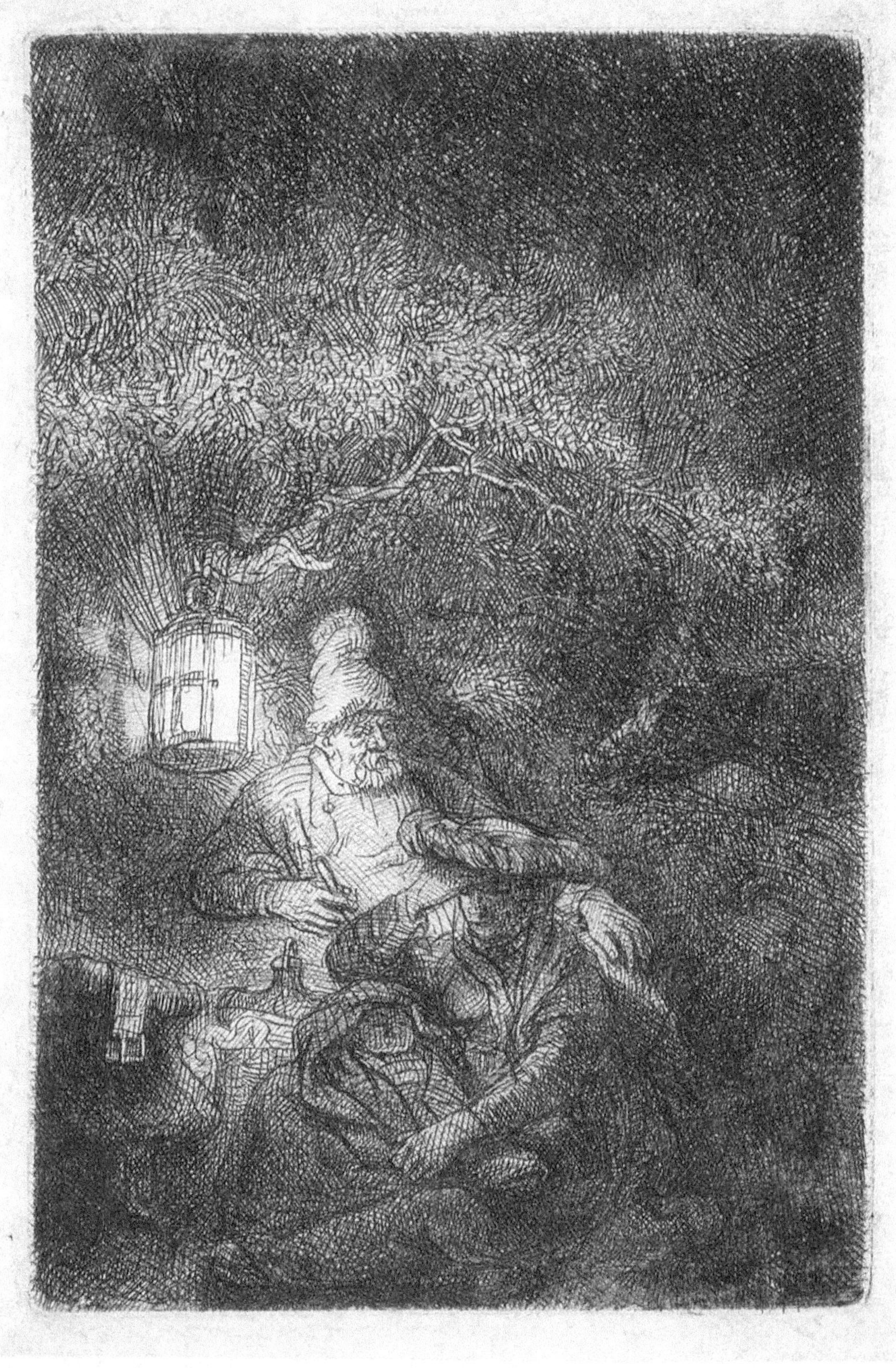

Rembrandt, The Rest on the Flight Into Egypt, Rijksmuseum, Amsterdam

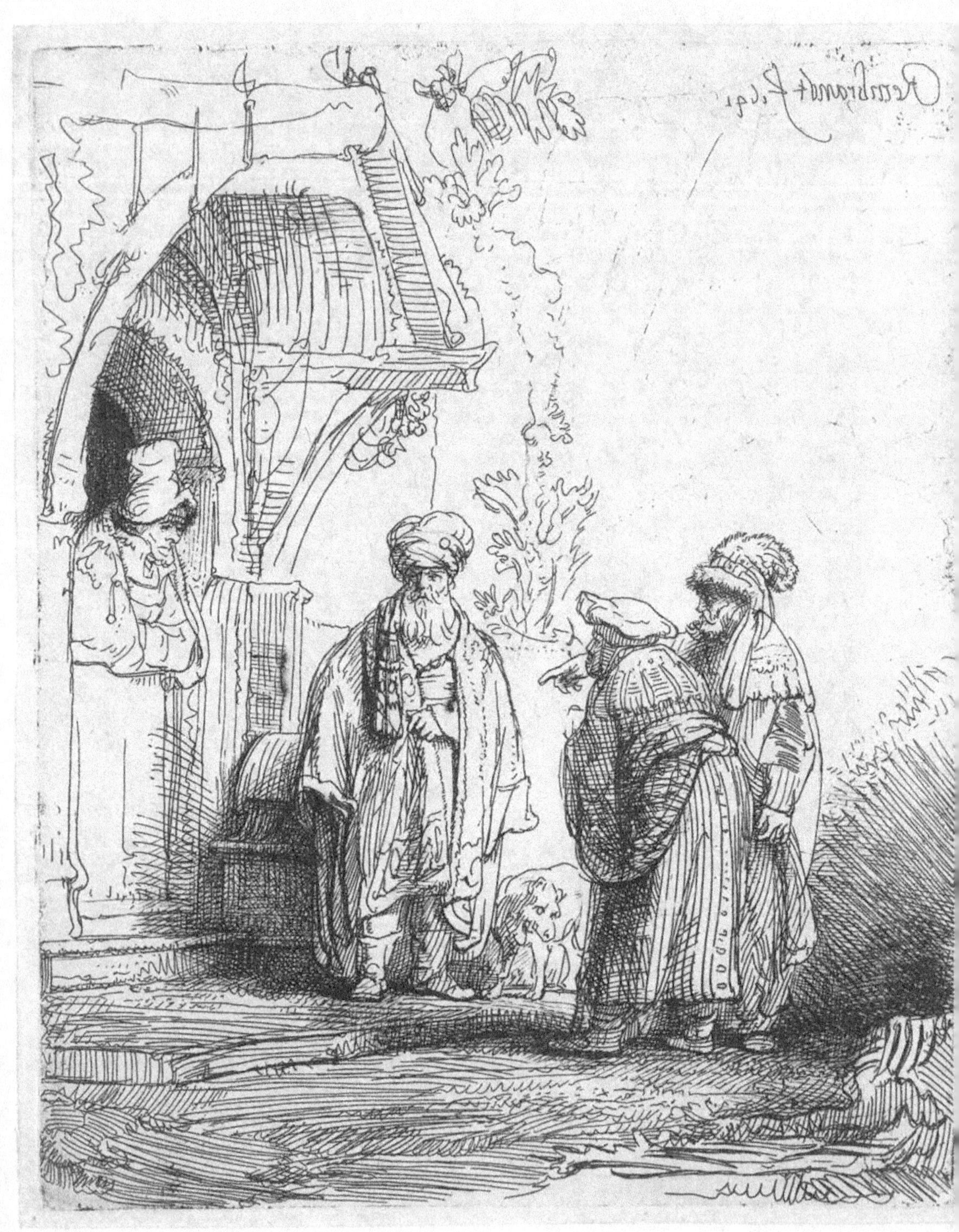

Rembrandt, Jacob and Laban, 1641, Rijksmuseum, Amsterdam

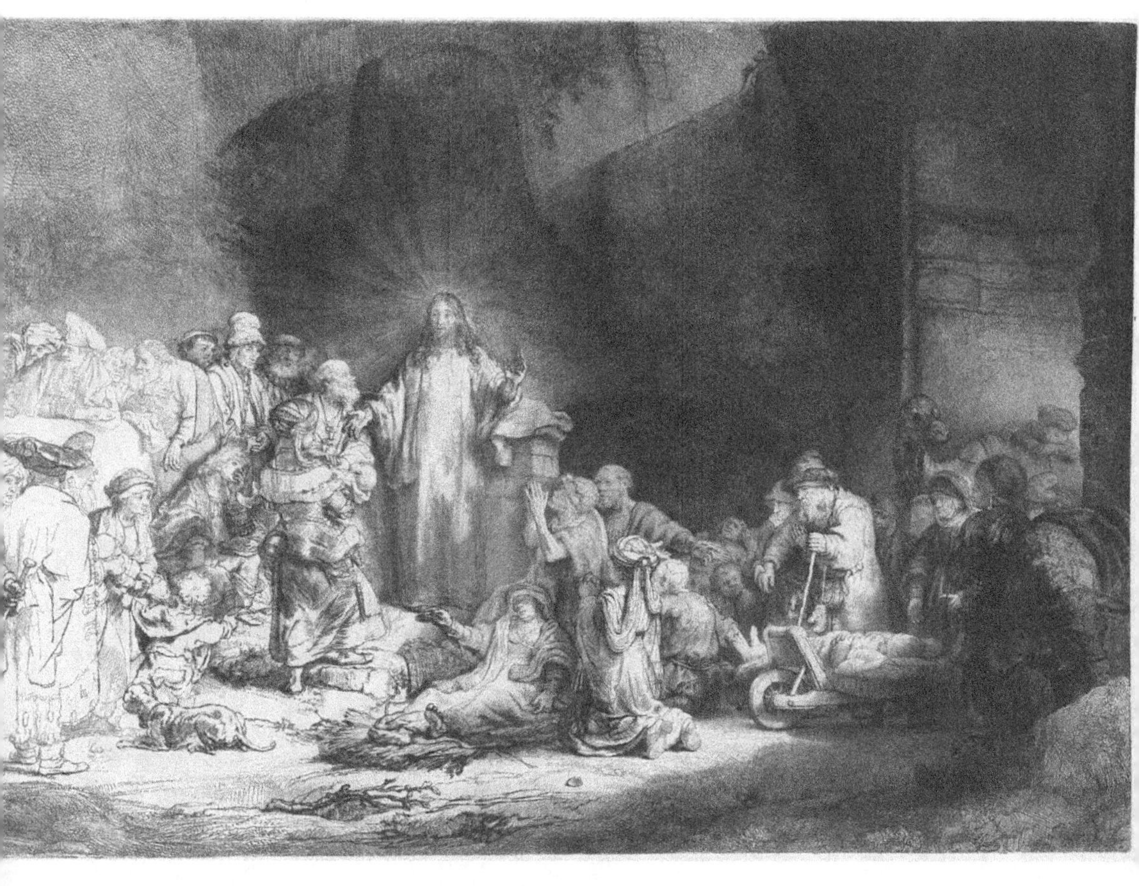

Rembrandt, The Little Children, 1646-50, Rijksmuseum, Amsterdam

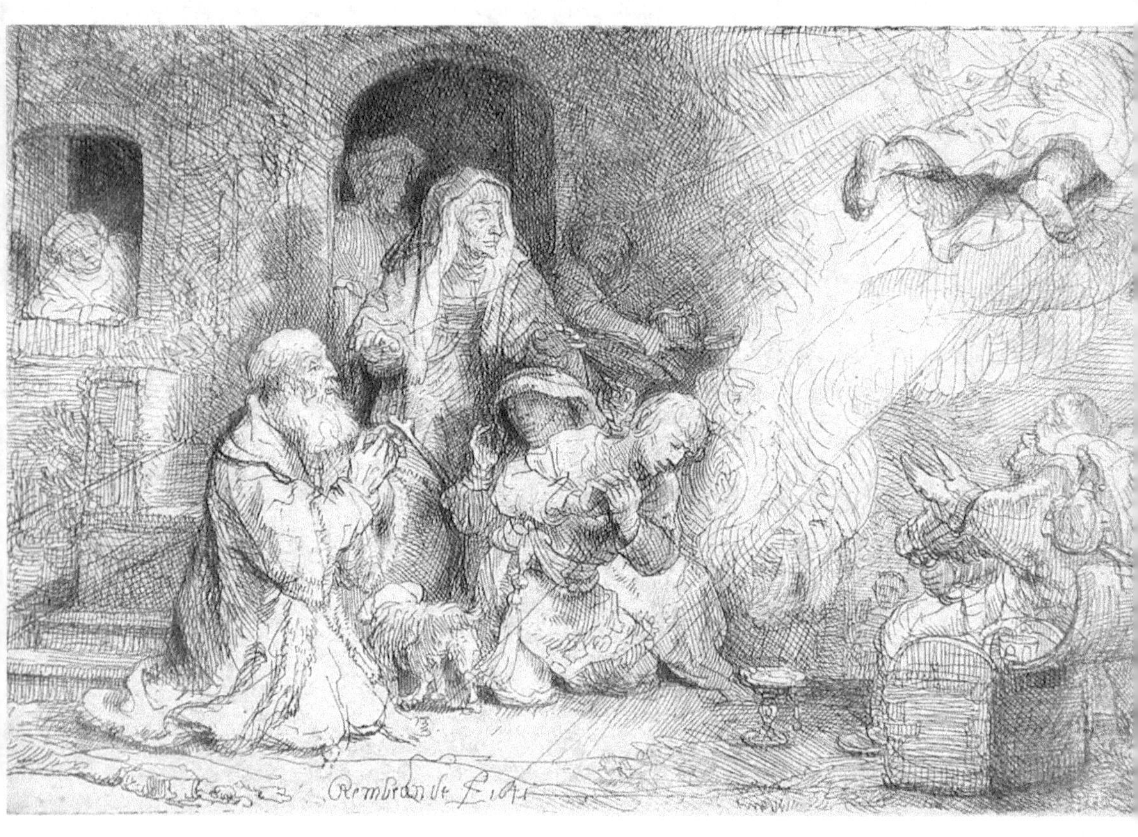

Rembrandt, The Angel Departing From the Family of Tobit, Los Angeles

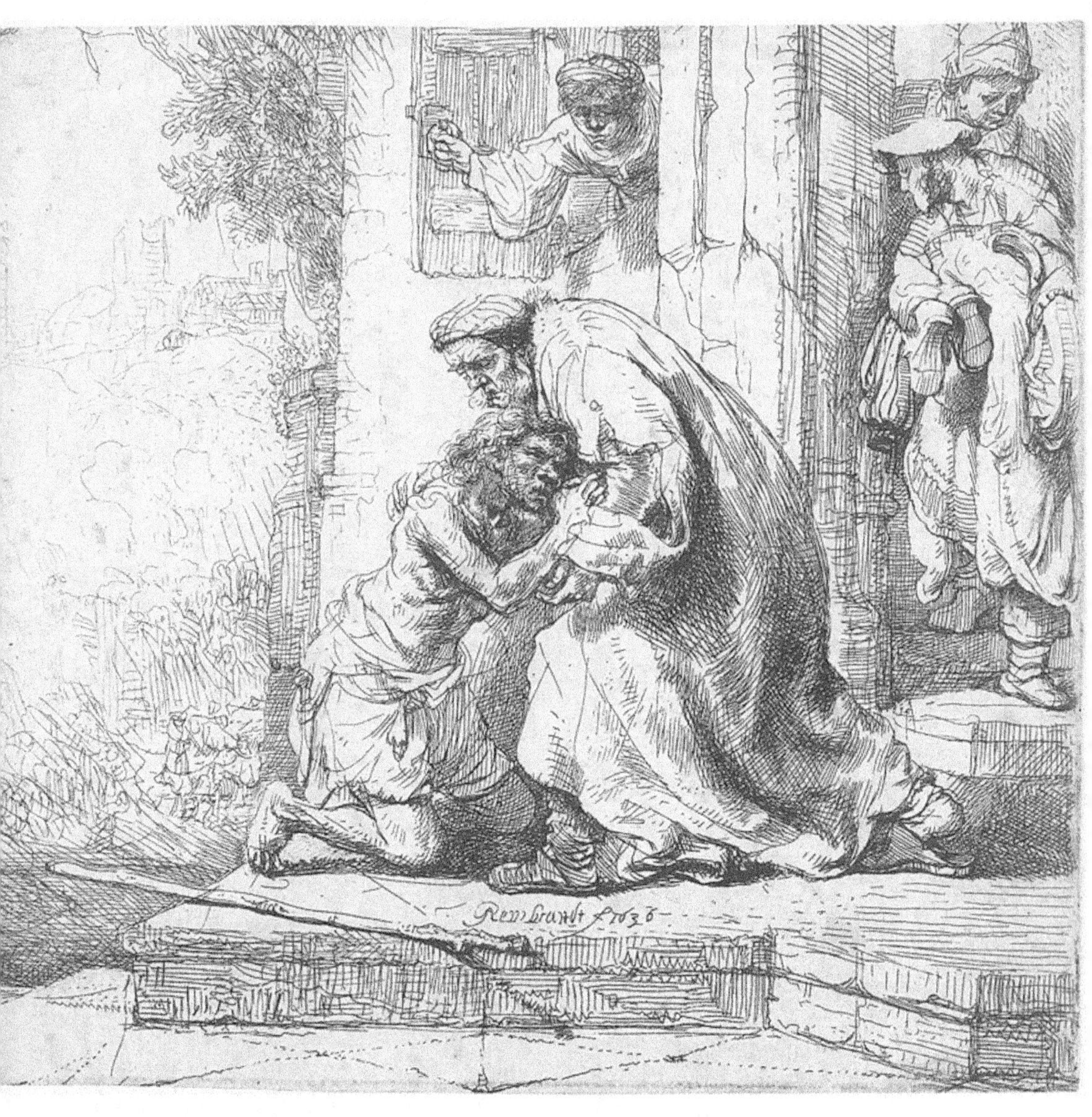

Rembrandt, The Return of the Prodigal Son, 1636, Rijksmuseum, Amsterdam

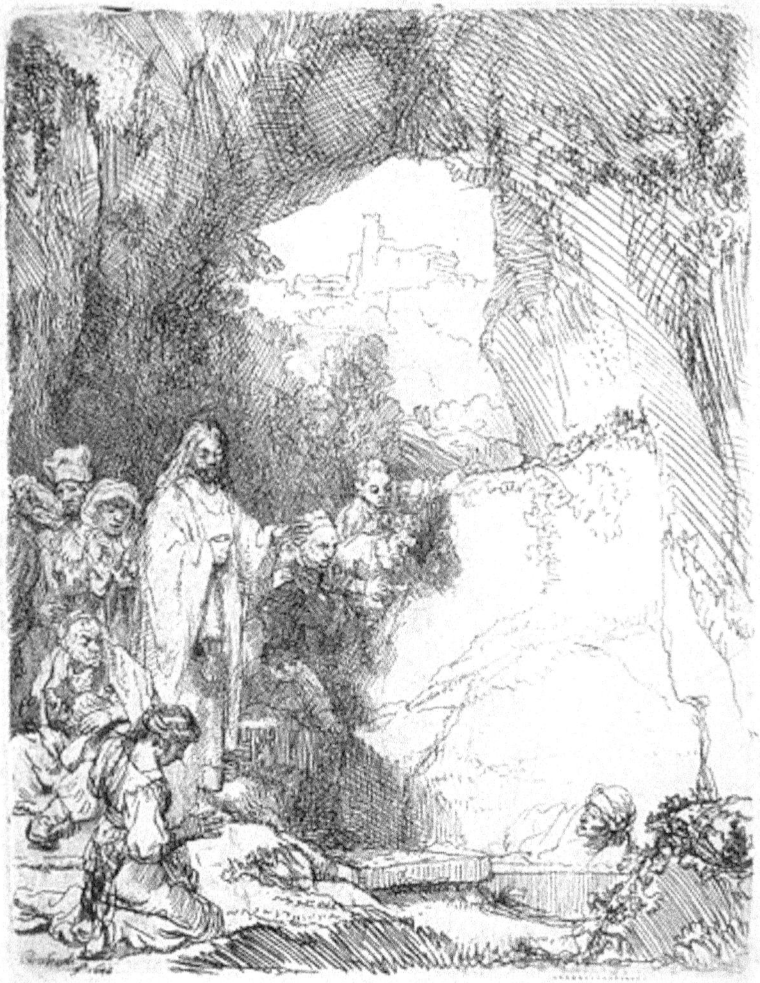

Rembrandt,
The Raising of Lazarus, 1642,
Rijksmuseum,
Amsterdam (above).
The Presentation In the
Temple, 1639,
British Museum (Right).

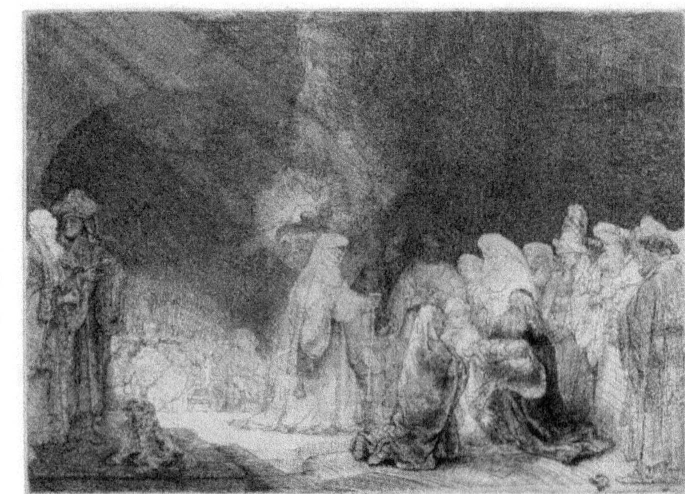

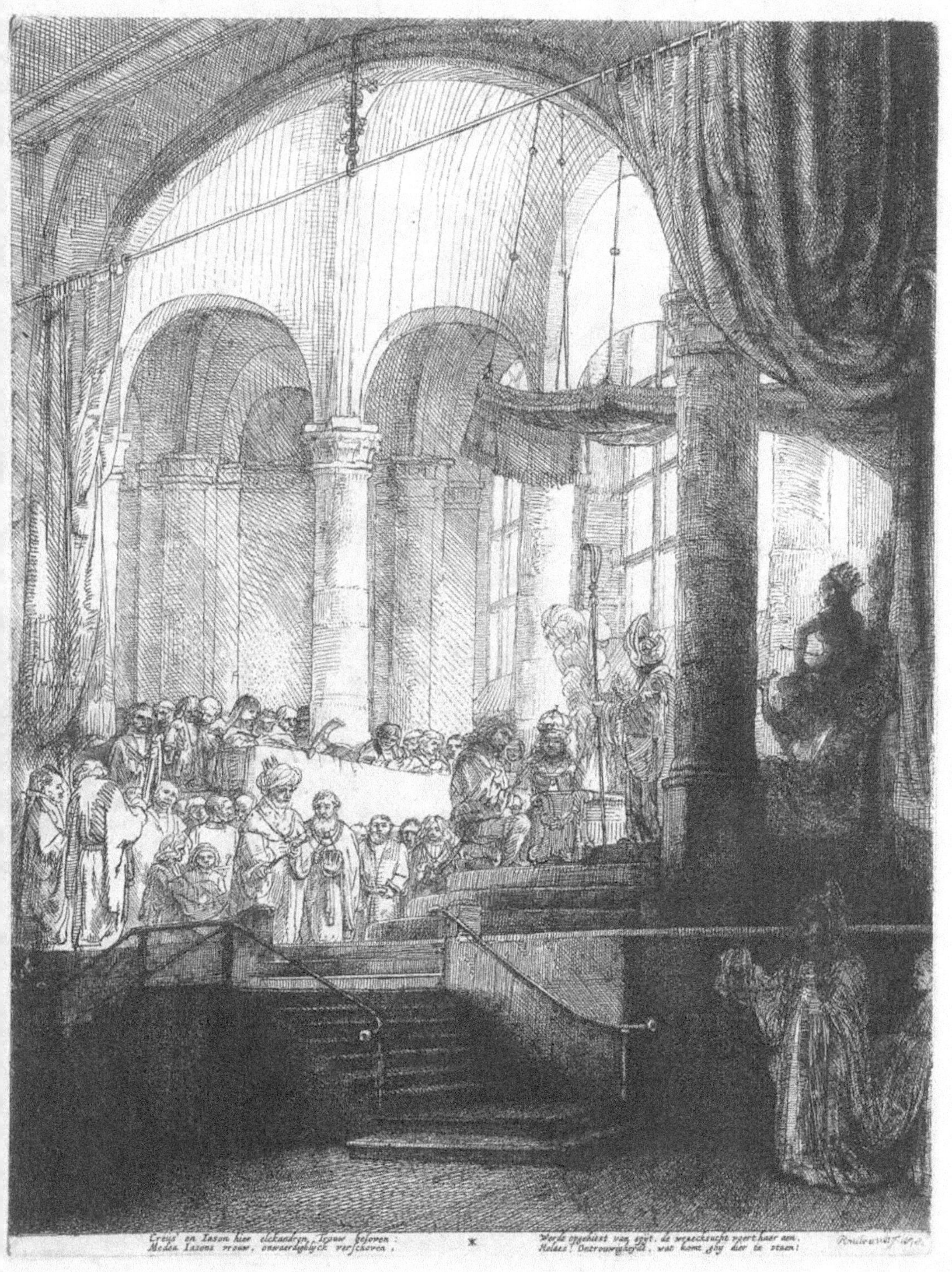

Rembrandt, Medea, 1648, Rijksmuseum, Amsterdam

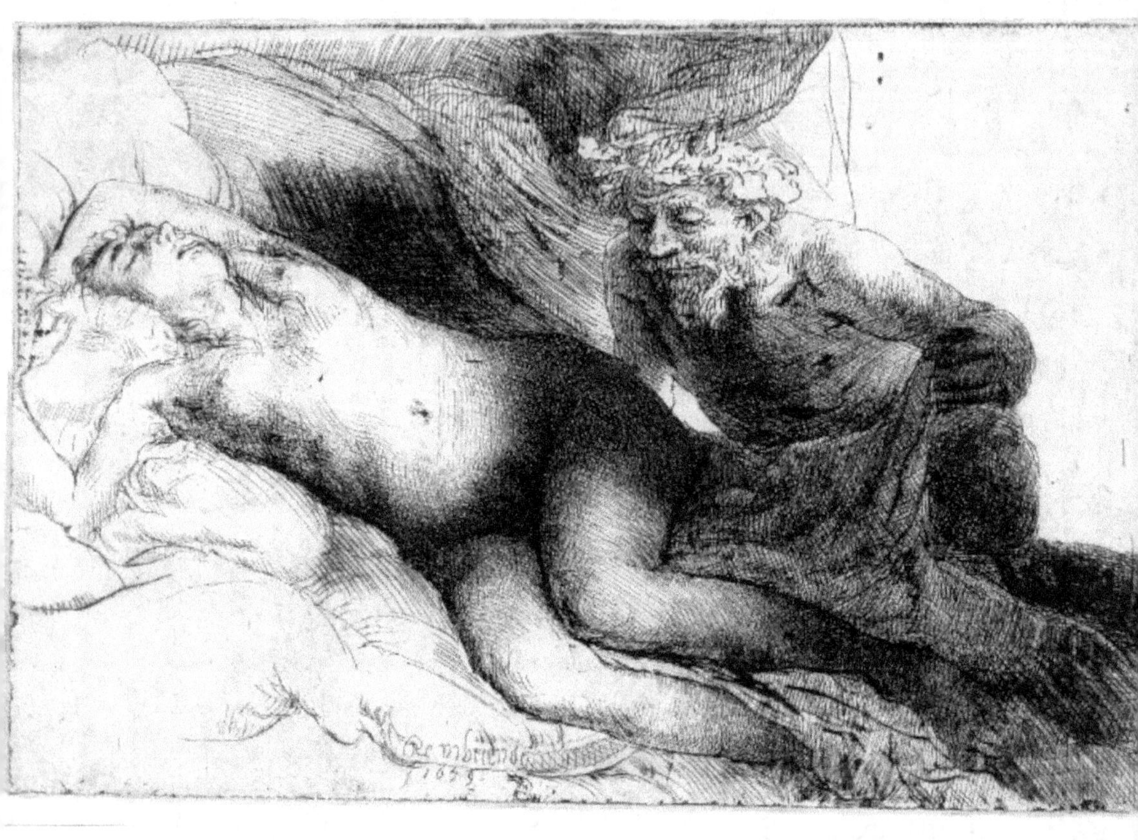

Rembrandt, Jupiter and Antiope, 1659, British Museum

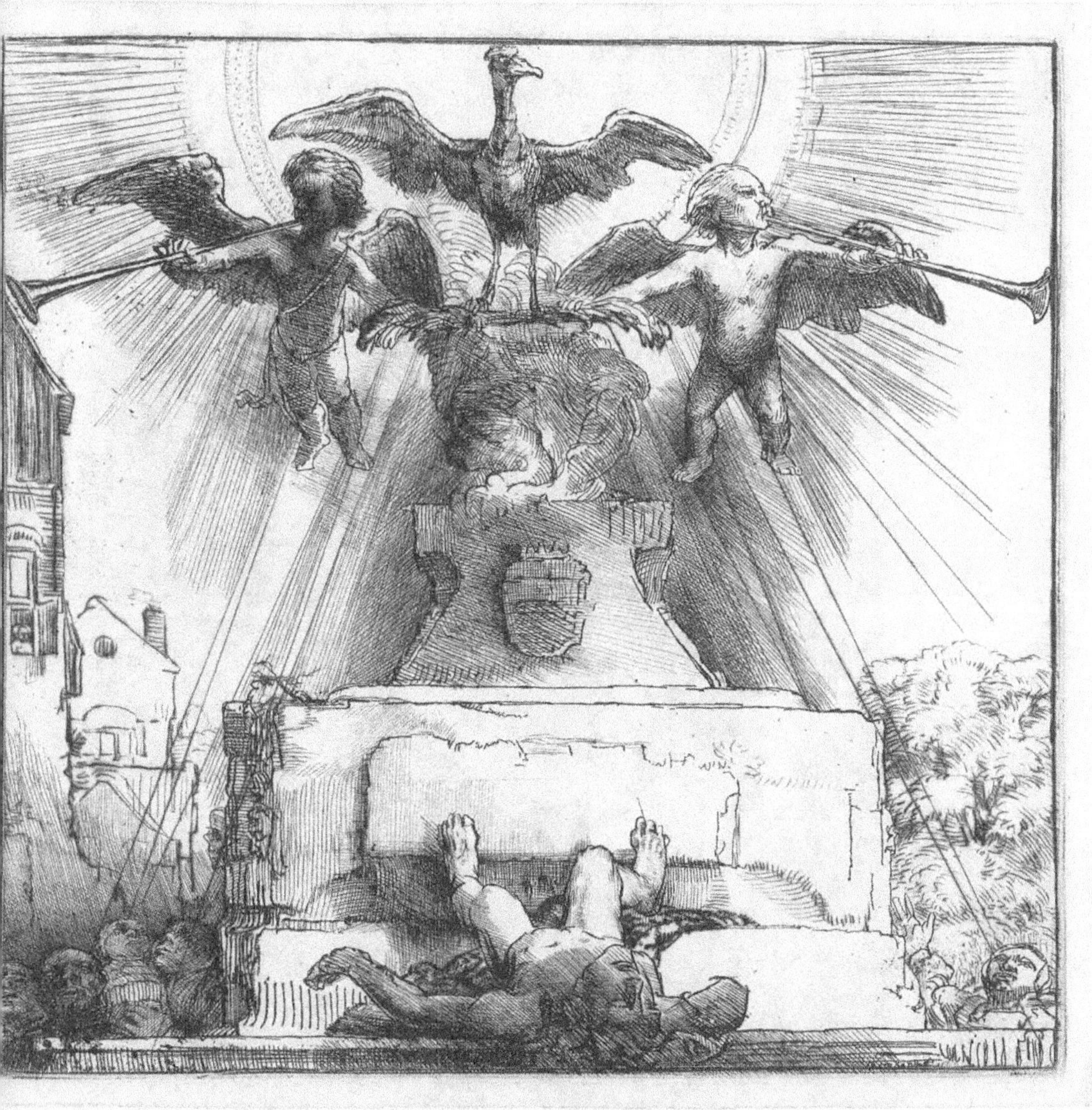

Rembrandt, The Phoenix, or the Statue Overthrown, 1658

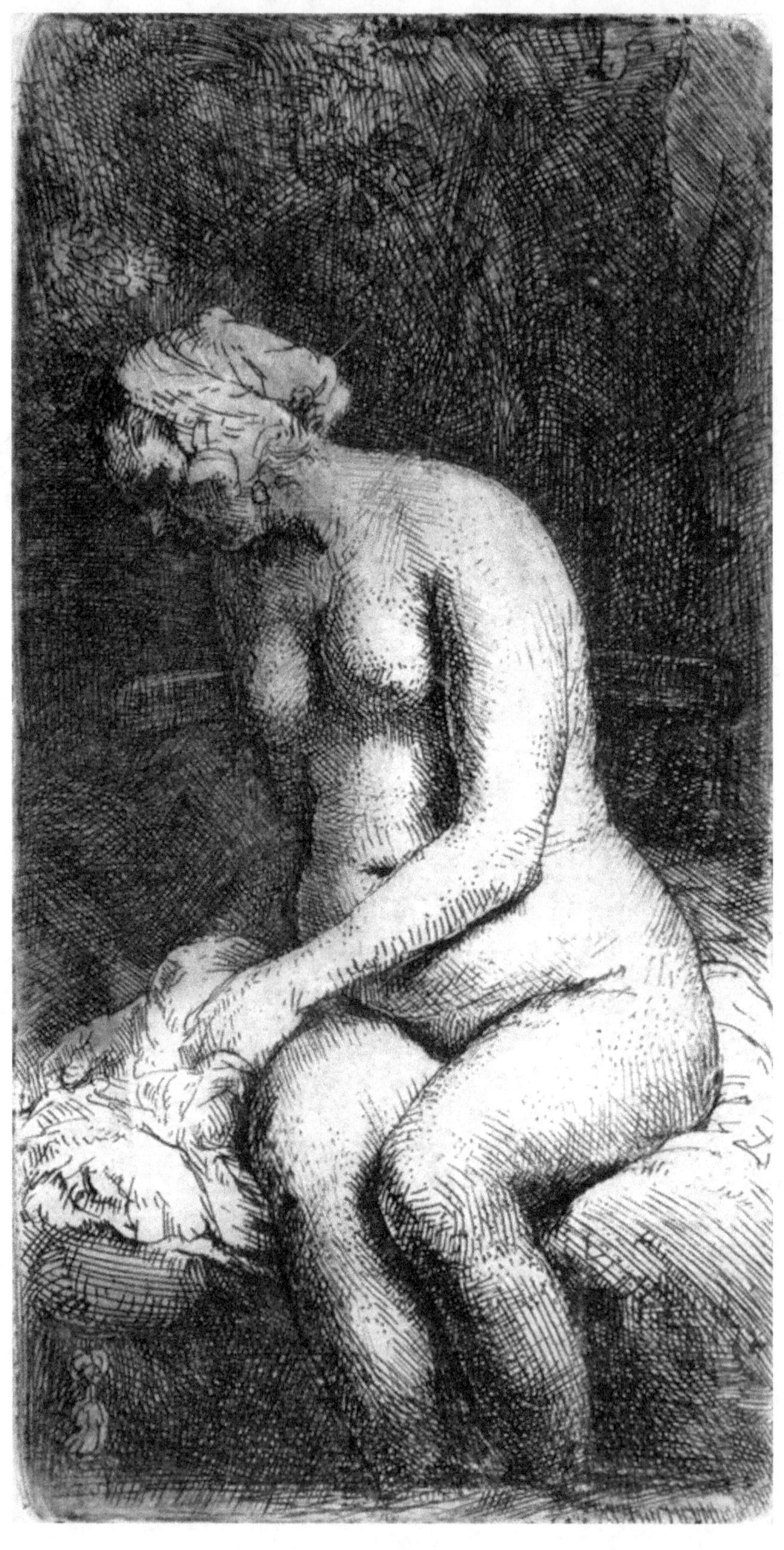

Rembrandt, Seated Nude, 1658

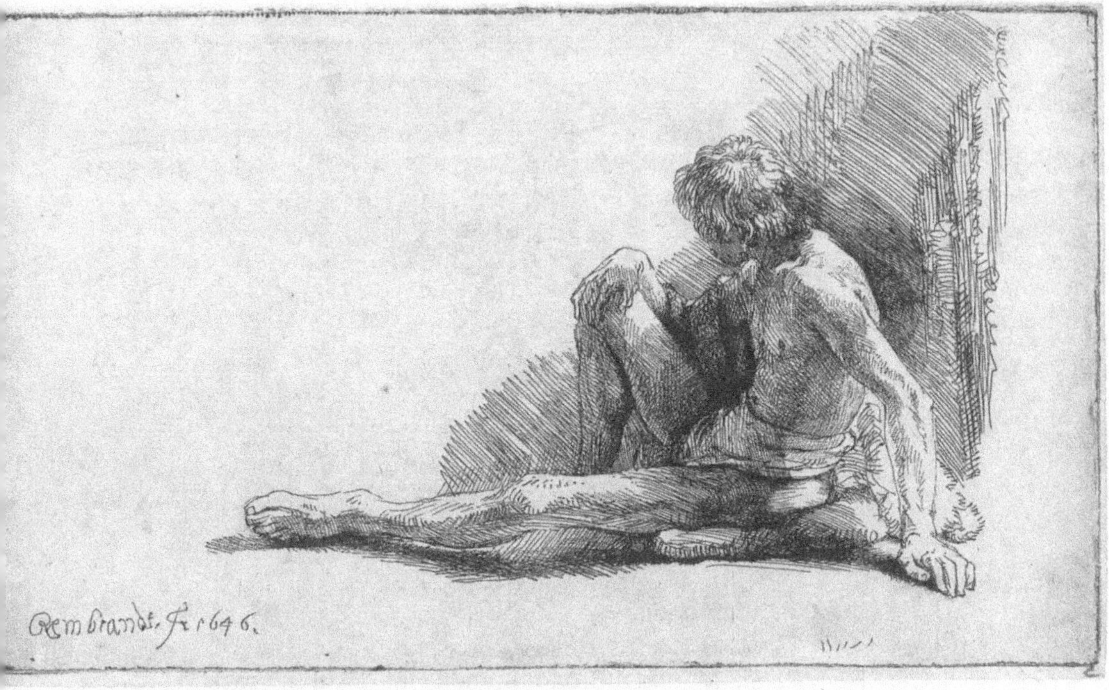

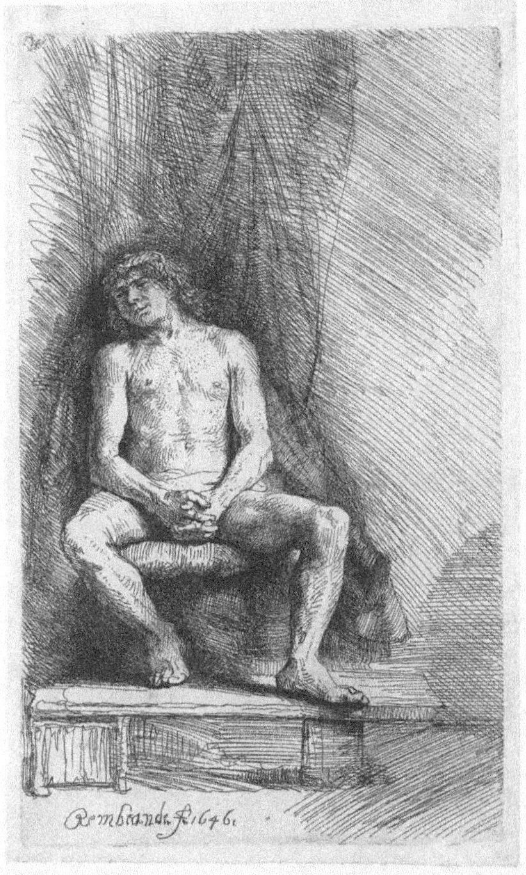

Rembrandt, Nude Man Seated,
1646 (above).
Nude Man Seated Before a Curtain,
Rijksmuseum, Amsterdam (left).

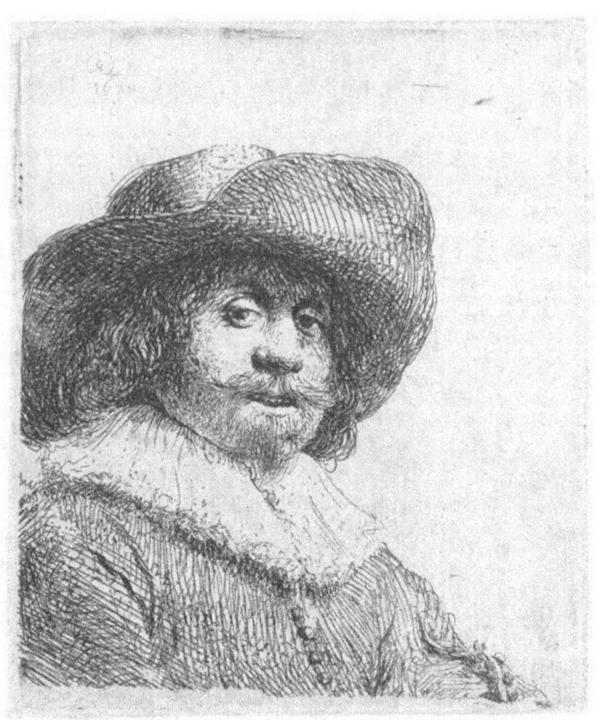

Rembrandt, Man In a Broad-rimmed Hat, 1638 (above).
Man At a Desk, 1641 (below). Both Rijksmuseum, Amsterdam.

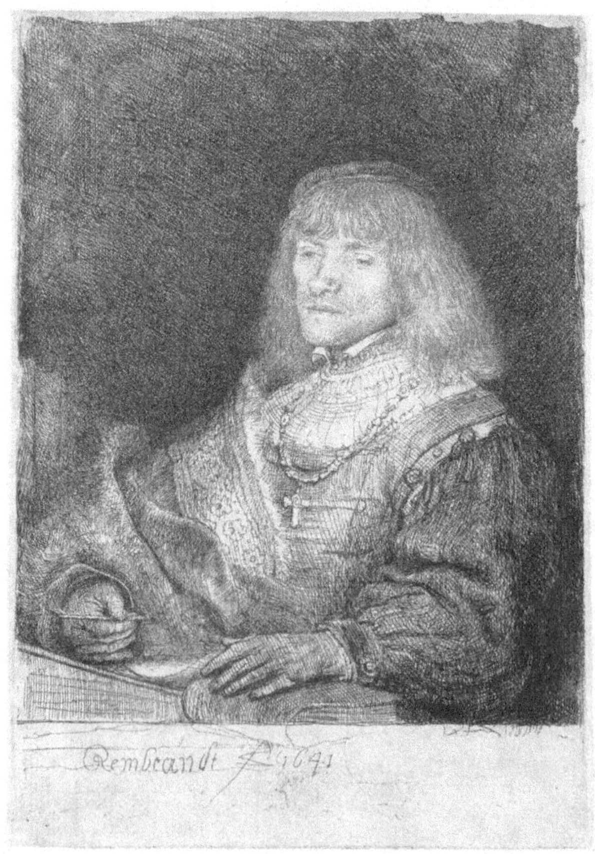

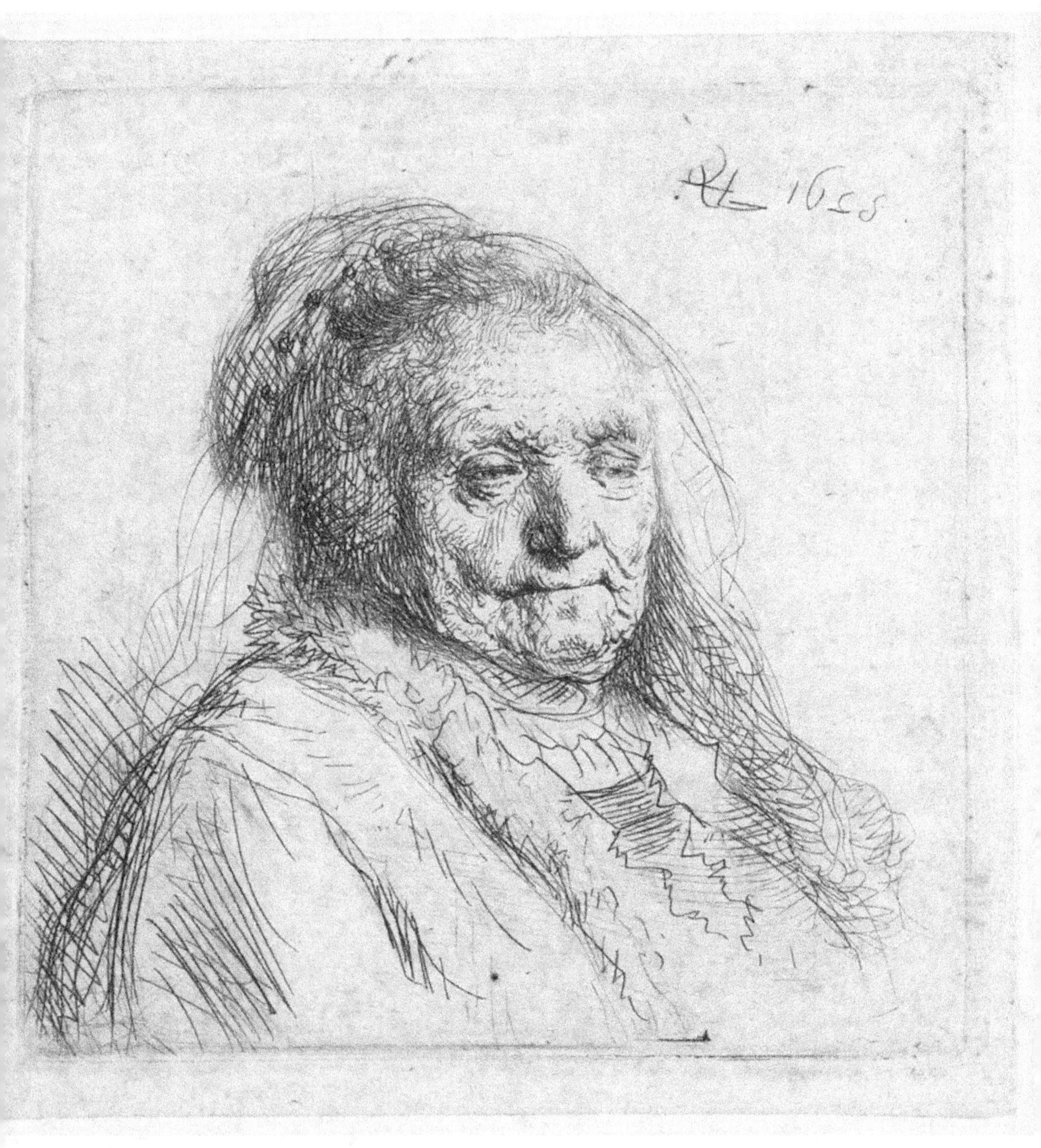

Rembrandt, Mother, 1628, Rijksmuseum, Amsterdam

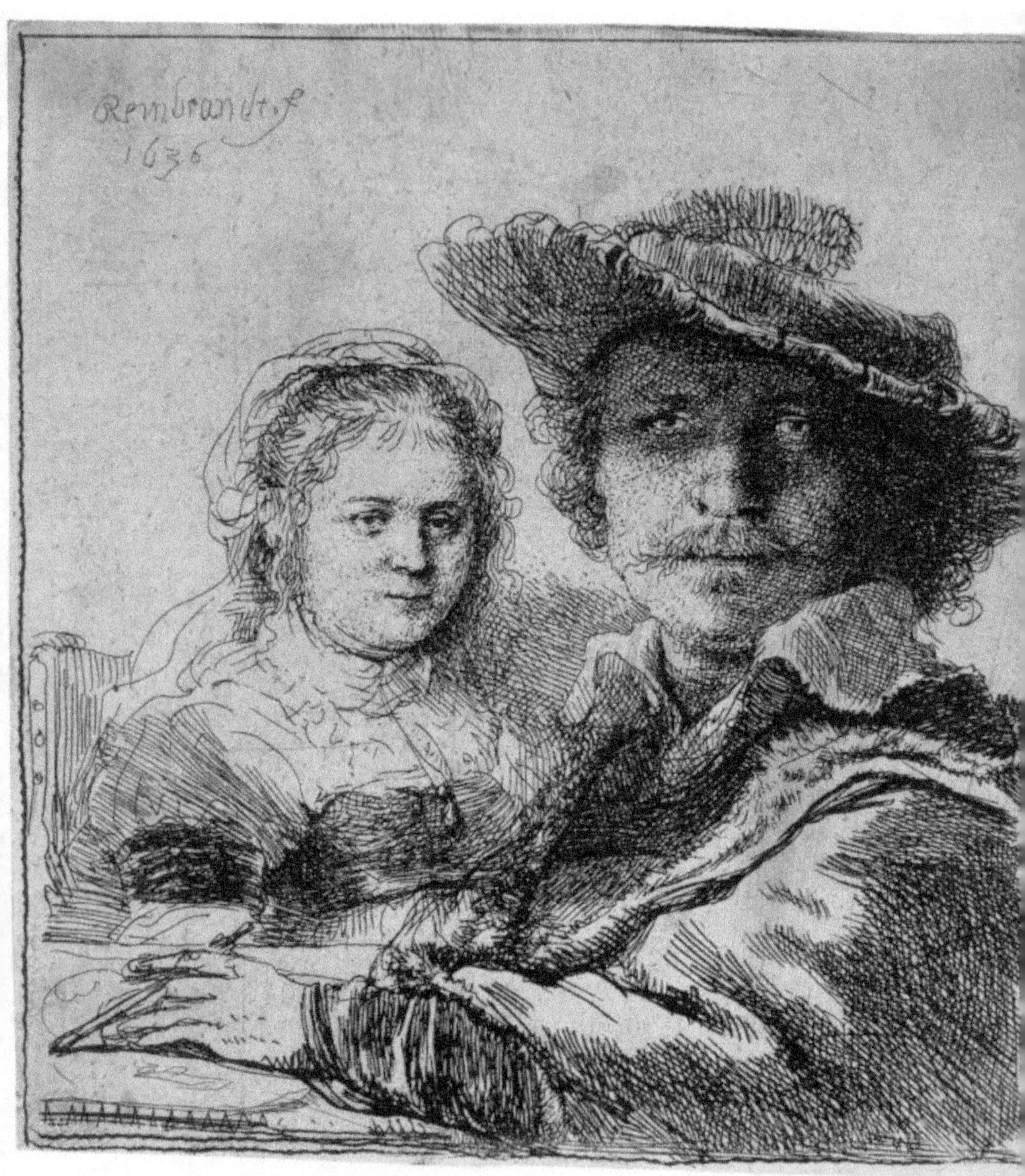

Rembrandt, Self-Portrait With Saskia, 1636, Hermitage Museum

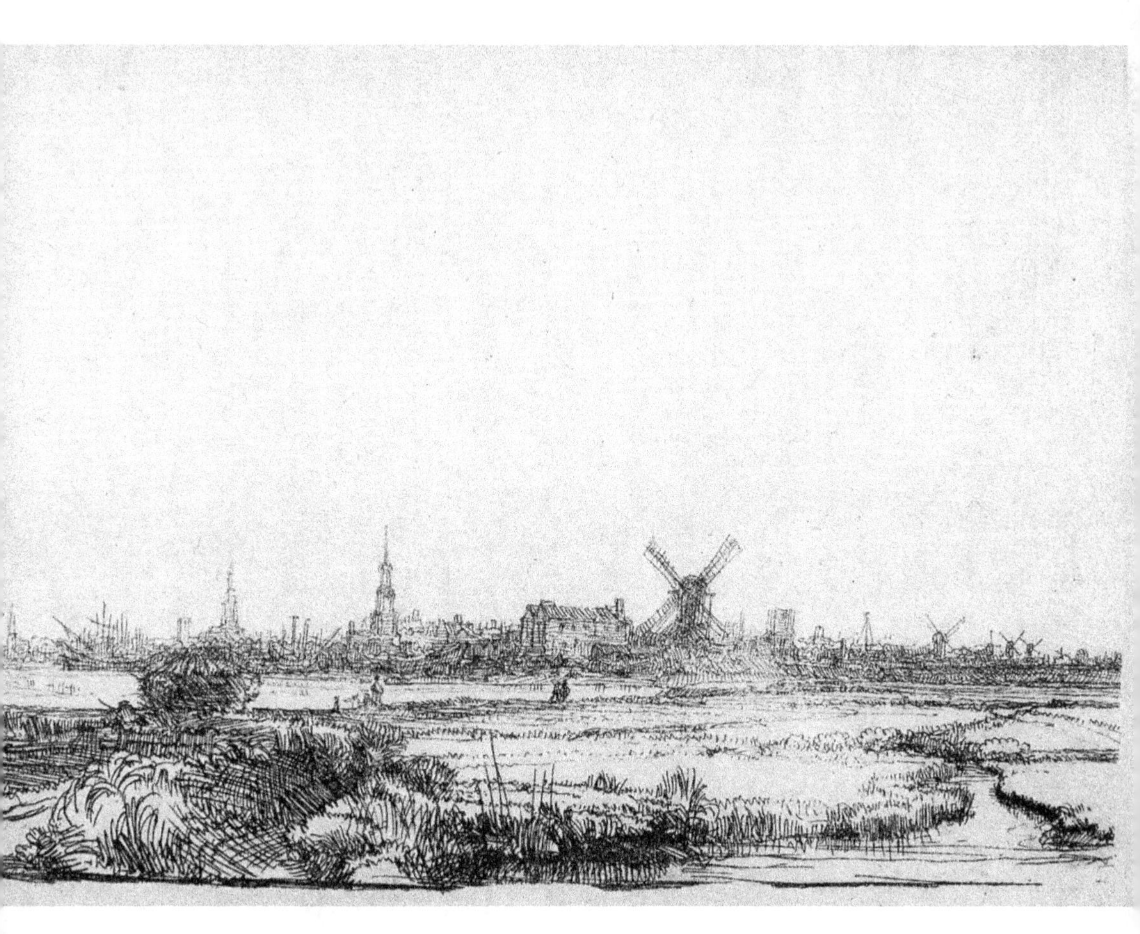

Rembrandt, Amsterdam, c. 1640

CRESCENT MOON PUBLISHING

web: www.crmoon.com e-mail: cresmopub@yahoo.co.uk

ARTS, PAINTING, SCULPTURE

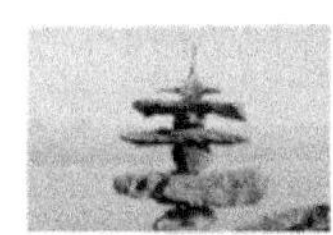
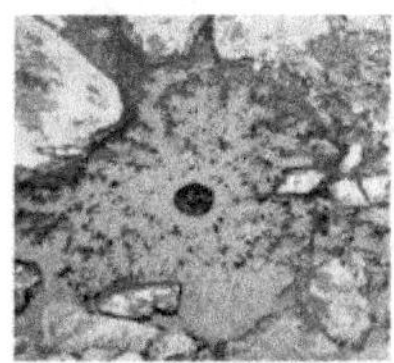

The Art of Andy Goldsworthy
Andy Goldsworthy: Touching Nature
Andy Goldsworthy in Close-Up
Andy Goldsworthy: Pocket Guide
Andy Goldsworthy In America
Land Art: A Complete Guide
The Art of Richard Long
Richard Long: Pocket Guide
Land Art In the UK
Land Art in Close-Up
Land Art In the U.S.A.

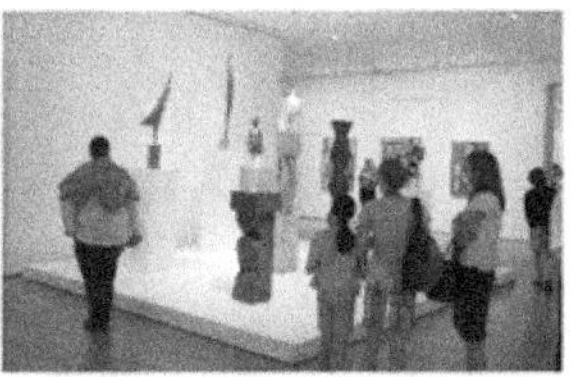
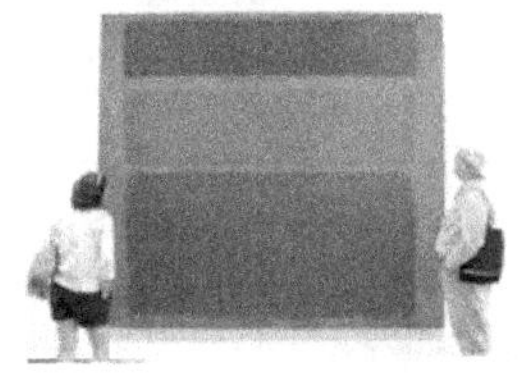

Land Art: Pocket Guide
Installation Art in Close-Up
Minimal Art and Artists In the 1960s and After
Colourfield Painting
Land Art DVD, TV documentary
Andy Goldsworthy DVD, TV documentary
The Erotic Object: Sexuality in Sculpture From Prehistory to the Present Day
Sex in Art: Pornography and Pleasure in Painting and Sculpture
Postwar Art
Sacred Gardens: The Garden in Myth, Religion and Art
Glorification: Religious Abstraction in Renaissance and 20th Century Art
Early Netherlandish Painting

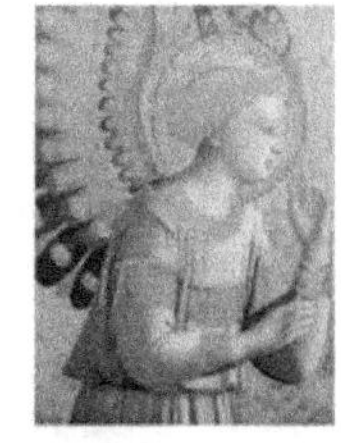

Leonardo da Vinci
Piero della Francesca
Giovanni Bellini
Fra Angelico: Art and Religion in the Renaissance
Mark Rothko: The Art of Transcendence
Frank Stella: American Abstract Artist

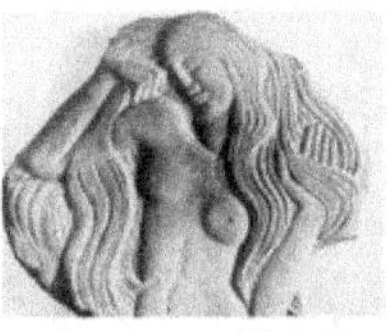
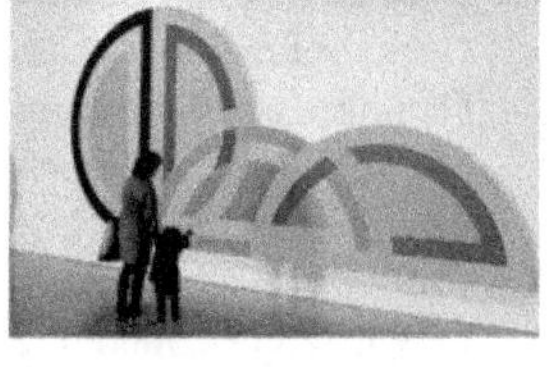

Jasper Johns
Brice Marden
Alison Wilding: The Embrace of Sculpture
Vincent van Gogh: Visionary Landscapes
Eric Gill: Nuptials of God

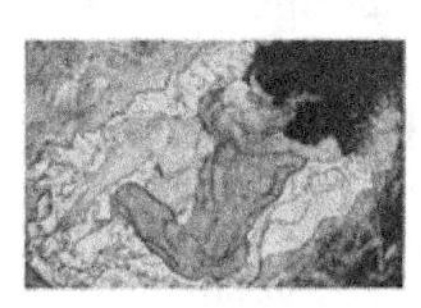
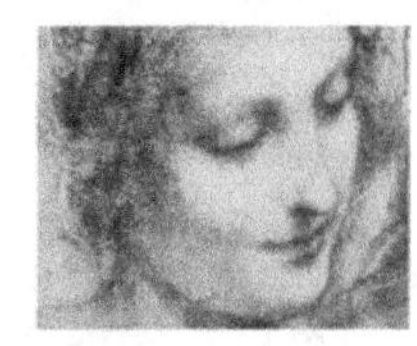

Constantin Brancusi: Sculpting the Essence of Things
Max Beckmann
Caravaggio
Gustave Moreau
Egon Schiele: Sex and Death In Purple Stockings
Delizioso Fotografico Fervore: Works In Process 1
Sacro Cuore: Works In Process 2
The Light Eternal: J.M.W. Turner
The Madonna Glorified: Karen Arthurs

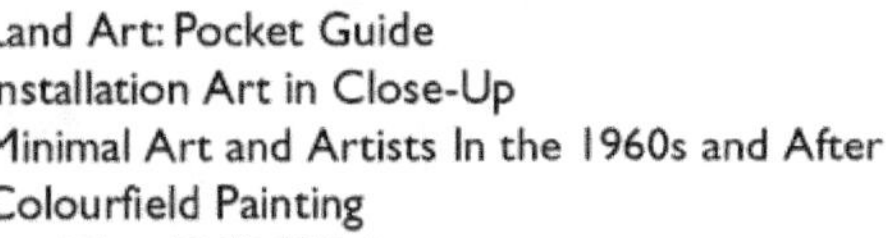
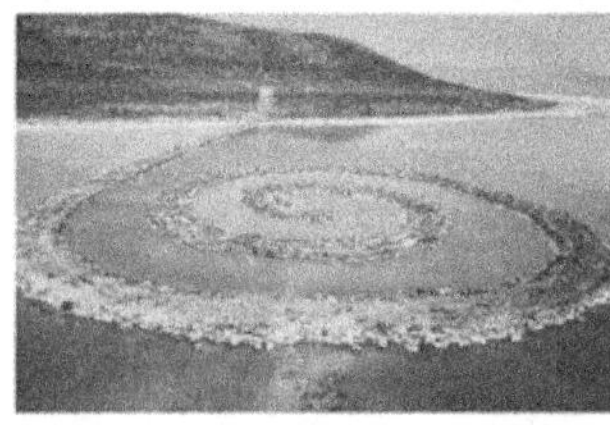

J.R.R. Tolkien: The Books, The Films, The Whole Cultural Phenomenon
J.R.R. Tolkien: Pocket Guide
Tolkien's Heroic Quest
The *Earthsea* Books of Ursula Le Guin
Beauties, Beasts and Enchantment: Classic French Fairy Tales
German Popular Stories by the Brothers Grimm
Philip Pullman and *His Dark Materials*
Sexing Hardy: Thomas Hardy and Feminism
Thomas Hardy's *Tess of the d'Urbervilles* 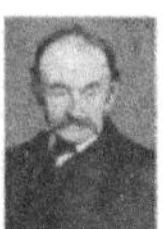 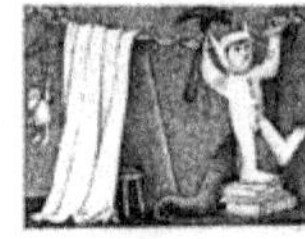
Thomas Hardy's *Jude the Obscure*
Thomas Hardy: The Tragic Novels
Love and Tragedy: Thomas Hardy
The Poetry of Landscape in Hardy
Wessex Revisited: Thomas Hardy and John Cowper Powys
Wolfgang Iser: Essays and Interviews 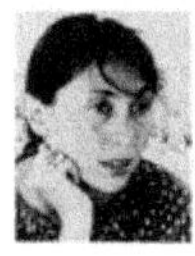
Petrarch, Dante and the Troubadours
Maurice Sendak and the Art of Children's Book Illustration
Andrea Dworkin 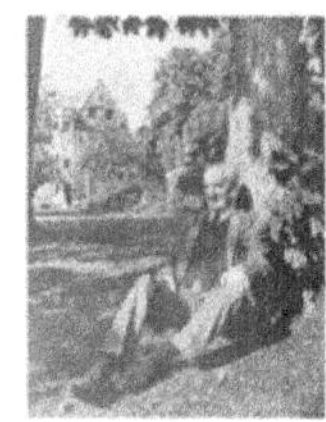
Cixous, Irigaray, Kristeva: The *Jouissance* of French Feminism
Julia Kristeva: Art, Love, Melancholy, Philosophy, Semiotics and Psychoanalysis
Hélene Cixous I Love You: The *Jouissance* of Writing
Luce Irigaray: Lips, Kissing, and the Politics of Sexual Difference
Peter Redgrove: Here Comes the Flood
Peter Redgrove: Sex-Magic-Poetry-Cornwall 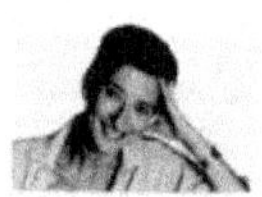
Lawrence Durrell: Between Love and Death, East and West
Love, Culture & Poetry: Lawrence Durrell
Cavafy: Anatomy of a Soul
German Romantic Poetry: Goethe, Novalis, Heine, Hölderlin
Feminism and Shakespeare
Shakespeare: Love, Poetry & Magic 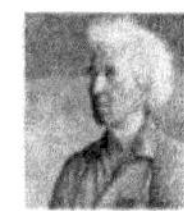
The Passion of D.H. Lawrence
D.H. Lawrence: Symbolic Landscapes 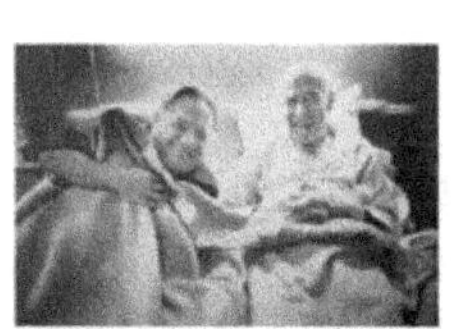
D.H. Lawrence: Infinite Sensual Violence
Rimbaud: Arthur Rimbaud and the Magic of Poetry
The Ecstasies of John Cowper Powys
Sensualism and Mythology: The Wessex Novels of John Cowper Powys
Amorous Life: John Cowper Powys and the Manifestation of Affectivity (H.W. Fawkner)
Postmodern Powys: New Essays on John Cowper Powys (Joe Boulter)
Rethinking Powys: Critical Essays on John Cowper Powys
Paul Bowles & Bernardo Bertolucci
Rainer Maria Rilke
Joseph Conrad: *Heart of Darkness* 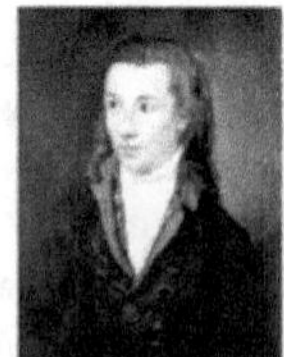
In the Dim Void: Samuel Beckett
Samuel Beckett Goes into the Silence
André Gide: Fiction and Fervour
Jackie Collins and the Blockbuster Novel
Blinded By Her Light: The Love-Poetry of Robert Graves
The Passion of Colours: Travels In Mediterranean Lands
Poetic Forms

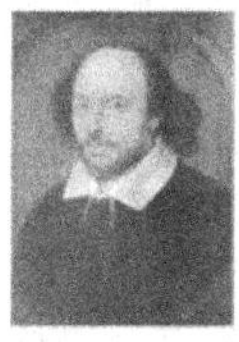
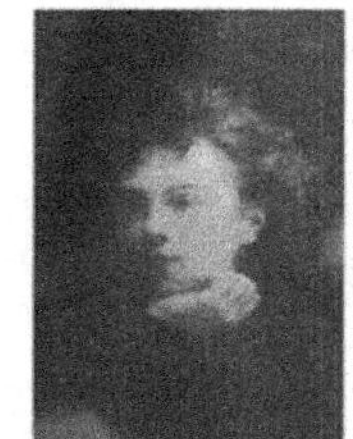
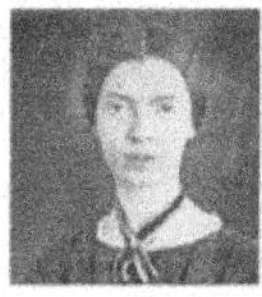
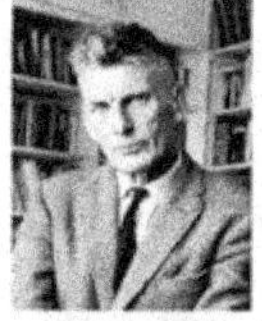
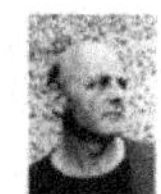
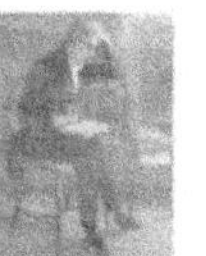
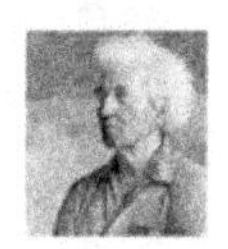
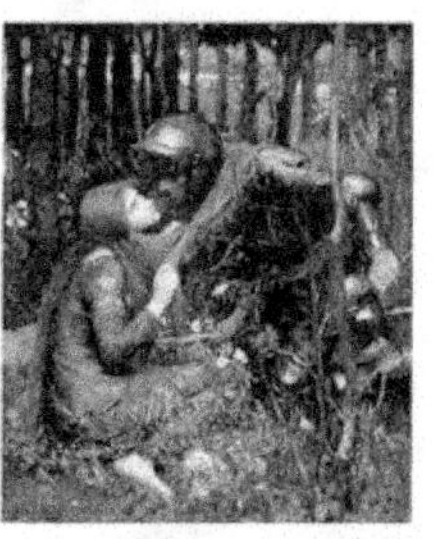
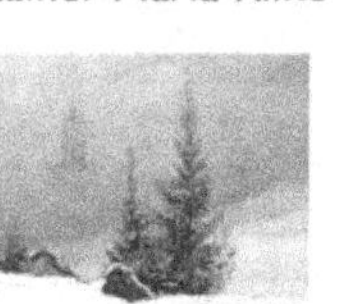
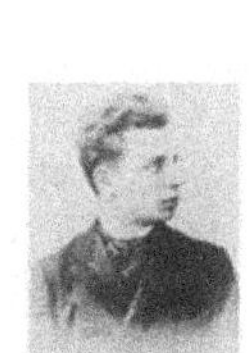
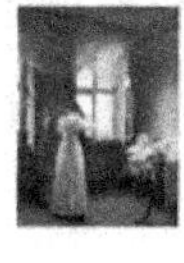
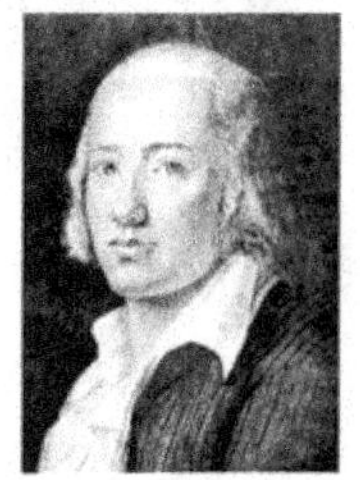
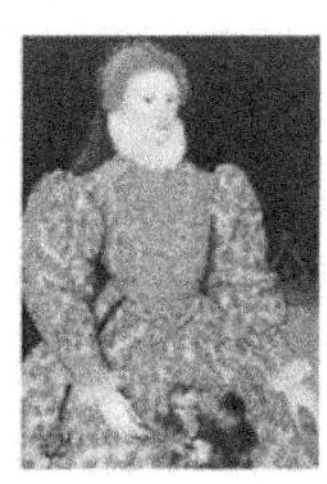

MEDIA, CINEMA, FEMINISM and CULTURAL STUDIES

J.R.R. Tolkien: The Books, The Films, The Whole Cultural Phenomenon
J.R.R. Tolkien: Pocket Guide
The *Lord of the Rings* Movies: Pocket Guide
The Cinema of Hayao Miyazaki
Hayao Miyazaki: *Princess Mononoke*: Pocket Movie Guide
Hayao Miyazaki: *Spirited Away*: Pocket Movie Guide
Tim Burton : Hallowe'en For Hollywood
Ken Russell

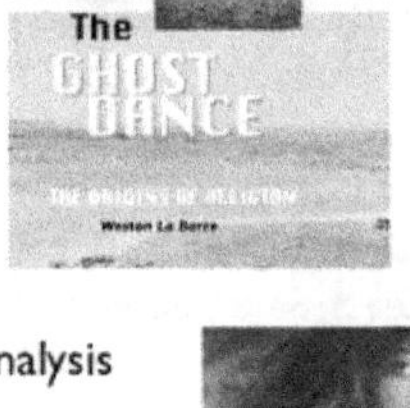

Ken Russell: *Tommy*: Pocket Movie Guide
The Ghost Dance: The Origins of Religion
The Peyote Cult
Cixous, Irigaray, Kristeva: The *Jouissance* of French Feminism
Julia Kristeva: Art, Love, Melancholy, Philosophy, Semiotics and Psychoanalysis
Luce Irigaray: Lips, Kissing, and the Politics of Sexual Difference
Hélene Cixous I Love You: The *Jouissance* of Writing
Andrea Dworkin

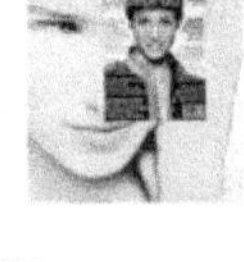
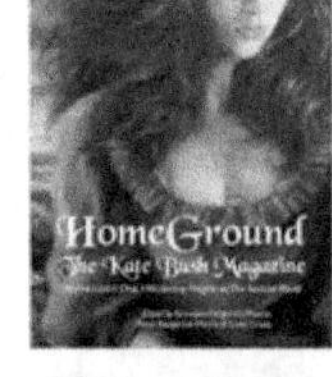

'Cosmo Woman': The World of Women's Magazines
Women in Pop Music
HomeGround: The Kate Bush Anthology
Discovering the Goddess (Geoffrey Ashe)
The Poetry of Cinema
The Sacred Cinema of Andrei Tarkovsky

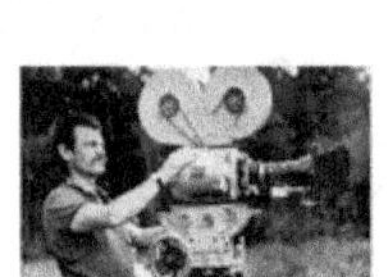
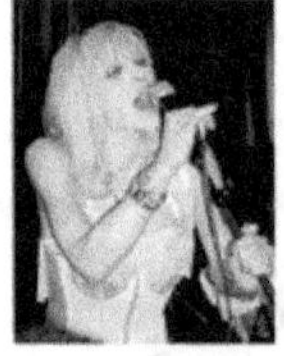

Andrei Tarkovsky: Pocket Guide
Andrei Tarkovsky: *Mirror*: Pocket Movie Guide
Andrei Tarkovsky: *The Sacrifice*: Pocket Movie Guide
Walerian Borowczyk: Cinema of Erotic Dreams
Jean-Luc Godard: The Passion of Cinema
Jean-Luc Godard: *Hail Mary*: Pocket Movie Guide

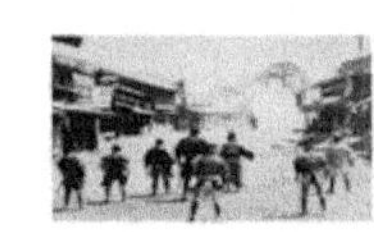
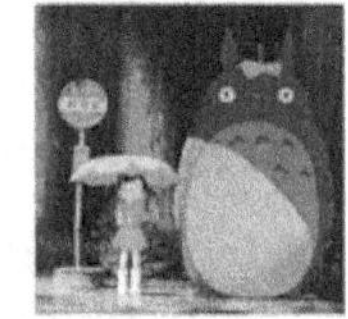

Jean-Luc Godard: *Contempt*: Pocket Movie Guide
Jean-Luc Godard: *Pierrot le Fou*: Pocket Movie Guide
John Hughes and Eighties Cinema
Ferris Bueller's Day Off: Pocket Movie Guide
Jean-Luc Godard: Pocket Guide
The Cinema of Richard Linklater

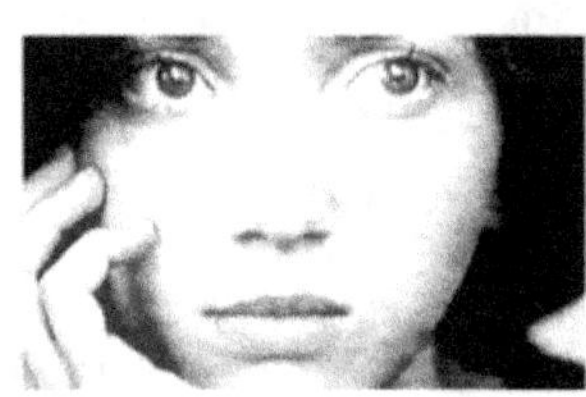

Liv Tyler: Star In Ascendance
Blade Runner and the Films of Philip K. Dick
Paul Bowles and Bernardo Bertolucci
Media Hell: Radio, TV and the Press
An Open Letter to the BBC
Detonation Britain: Nuclear War in the UK
Feminism and Shakespeare
Wild Zones: Pornography, Art and Feminism
Sex in Art: Pornography and Pleasure in Painting and Sculpture
Sexing Hardy: Thomas Hardy and Feminism

The Light Eternal is a model monograph, an exemplary job. The subject matter of the book is beautifully organised and dead on beam. (Lawrence Durrell)
It is amazing for me to see my work treated with such passion and respect. (Andrea Dworkin)

CRESCENT MOON PUBLISHING
P.O. Box 1312, Maidstone, Kent, ME14 5XU, Great Britain. www.crmoon.com

cresmopub@yahoo.co.uk   www.crescentmoon.org.uk